What Matters Most

THOUGHTS
ON A LIFE
WELL LIVED

All the Best!

Danny

DANNY KITTINGER

Praise for *What Matters Most*

If living well matters genuinely to you, then *What Matters Most* is a must-read! Danny Kittinger says he's an ordinary person, and I reckon it's true. Yet, his earnest disciplined attention to the Word of God and to Jesus, the Word that became flesh, has given his life form and substance, producing an extraordinarily enviable life. I'm confident it won't take long for you to trust his voice and be encouraged to, like him, "live a life that matters, and ultimately, for what matters most."

> Fil Anderson
> Spiritual Director, Conference Speaker,
> Retreat Leader and Author

I have known Danny since the 1970s when his family moved to Biloxi, Mississippi and we immediately became friends. I was impressed with the love that this whole family showed everyone they met. I watched as Dan grew physically and spiritually. Our families were very close, so I got to be around Dan a lot. We sang together, played ball together, fished and hunted together, so I got to watch Danny up close and personal. He was always honest to his Christian commitment.

It has been years since we moved apart, so I had no idea that Danny would write something this special. One of my favorite parts was about keeping it simple. This book is a great book to help remind us of things we should probably already know, but it is put together so well that anyone can profit from reading.

> Richard Black
> Music Pastor, Retired

I've always enjoyed reading about people's experiences. When well-told, they have a way of transporting me into their story where I feel what they feel and, as if by magic, I gain the same experience they did. Danny's book *What Matters Most* did that for me. But there is something about this book that surprised me. I saw Danny's story inside a larger story, one that is shared by all of us. Though Danny's story is not mine, I found myself saying over and over, "Yes, that's my story too!" That's when it hit me . . . there is really only one story, the only one that will continue into eternity. It's God's story played out in each of us like a grand symphony. Danny's. Mine. Yours. Each chapter was like a mile marker to me, written with Danny's sweat, tears, and blood over a lifetime of faithfulness to his God. I read this book slowly, putting it down after each chapter and used it as a measure in my own life. I was blessed, and you will be too—not just for its wisdom, but from the discovery that you are on the same journey, being prepared for what matters most—our eternal home with Jesus.

Pete Blum
Pastor, CPA and Real Estate Professional

Living a life of insignificance is not a goal for most people—discovering how to live a life that matters is! In *What Matters Most,* Danny offers us a fresh road map on how we may live in a unique and reviving way even if we are fatigued by the journey of life that sometimes feels like it's only uphill.

Joseph Bojang
Marketing Strategist, JosephBojang.com

STOP . . . are you tired of the "same old same old?" It's time to reset, renew, and revive what matters most in your life. This book was birthed in the heart of a guy I've had the honor of working with on a daily basis for nearly thirty years. I greatly respect what he has to say. If you're ready to reset your priorities, renew your life's purpose, and revive the areas in your life that matter most, you've got the right book in your hands. SO, DON'T PUT IT DOWN . . . READ IT! Live intentionally . . . focus on what matters most!

Rick Fenimore
President and Managing Member of TCIX Rail

Speaking as a thirty-year friend and a colleague, I can say Danny has indeed lived life well. Through life's ups and downs as well as unexpected twists and turns, he has navigated life in a manner worthy of emulating. We can all learn something from him. I hope you enjoy the read as much as I have.

Terry Fisher

CEO and Managing Member of TCIX Rail

Years ago, I sat with my dear friend Danny Kittinger and asked him to help me answer a difficult question, "Can a Christian know with clarity what they should be up to at any given moment?" Danny answered in his honest voice and as the honest man that he is, "Boy, Shea, that is a tall order. I am not sure." In an incredible writing voice, he has indeed answered that question. But not in the way I was hoping or expecting. He simply offers a playbook and glimpse into his journey of deciding what matters most.

If you had the pleasure of knowing Danny, you would find congruence, integrity, and a longing for more out of life. Read this book. Let it help you settle down. Wrestle with what he wrestles with. These really are lifelong mysteries that deserve our full attention. In doing so, like me, you will get real insight on making the next right decisions.

I have the highest praise for the truths in this book. Bless you on your journey to discover what matters most.

Shea Fite

Realtor at Skyline Realty, LLC and owner of

WhiteTree Company, LLC

I have known Danny Kittinger for almost thirty years. His book, *What Matters Most,* is a compilation of my experiences and observations of his life, marriage, and family. Danny exemplifies a "life well-lived" and his book weaves a beautiful tapestry of personal experiences, scripture, and insight. Like railroad tracks, Danny's heartfelt exposition of fifteen simple principles lays out the ties and rails the cars of a meaningful life should ride upon.

The book is a refreshing call to the core values of life, love, and relationship. It is a read tuned to the pure note of simplicity, and in the cacophony of a culture filled with distraction and fruitless pursuits, it refreshes the soul. I am proud of my friend and I know that *What Matters Most* will be a fulfilling and restorative read for anyone seeking to live with purpose and meaning in their life.

> Roger Gerstenberger
> Head of Schools,
> Northwestern Christian Schools, Inc.

What Matters Most gives the reader a treasure of wisdom for living a rich and full life. With engaging personal stories and inspiring quotes, each chapter is worth mulling over. This is a book you can read several times and refer back to for guidance in how to live the best kind of life.

> Dave Jewitt
> Founder, Your One Degree

This is not a "how-to" book. This is a "follow me as I follow Christ" book. This is not the work of a theologian, delivering a studied, referenced, sequential treatise on how we should strive to live right. This is the work of a God-follower, adventurer, and traveling companion, encouraging us along the journey to seize the day. There are no signposts here, pointing out the specific turns to take along the road. But there are abundant insights to help us interpret the landscape, match the map to the terrain, and keep placing one foot in front of the other with confidence.

If there is one chapter from the book that exemplifies what I know of my brother, it's the chapter on simplicity. Danny has simply loved, served, and encouraged me all my life! I fully expect this little gem will do the same for you.

> Greg Kittinger
> Labor Relations Institute

My friend, Danny, has written a wonderful testament to the pursuit of holiness across multiple generations. A fruitful read for those needing some encouragement that the daily habits of wisdom will profoundly impact your family and community in a frayed 21st century.

McCrary "Mac" Lowe
Principal / Portfolio Manager at
Gibraltar Capital Management

I've been friends with Danny Kittinger for more than thirty years and witnessed his well-lived life. The two of us have had plenty of great lunches and conversations. In every interaction, our words always return to what matters most. His insights and encouragement leave me better each time we meet. In this outstanding book, he reveals to you his wisdom that I have experienced firsthand. That's why I'm thrilled to endorse *What Matters Most*. I promise it will help you attain what matters most in your life and relationships.

John Mason
Author of *An Enemy Called Average* and
numerous other best-selling books

This book, *What Matters Most*, is a must-read for anyone wanting to expand their influence and effectiveness as a leader of their home, workplace, church, and community. Danny Kittinger does an excellent job identifying fifteen areas of our lives that truly matter, starting with the position of our heart and ending with Jesus—the author and finisher of our faith. As he says in the book, "The world needs ordinary people to live lives that matter, lives that make a difference." You will realize by reading this book that the most important things in life aren't money, fame, or popularity. But instead, it's understanding that God created you for a purpose and to have an identity found in him; to experience his goodness and grace, and to disciple others on what matters most. After reading this book, you won't look at life the same way as you did before. It'll change your mindsets and the daily decisions you make, I assure you.

Brad J. Pepin
Founder & CEO – Pepin Capital Group, LLC

I have known Danny personally for over thirty years and can attest to his outstanding character and authentic love for Jesus, his family, and his friends. I found the following statement early in the book to be inspiring and encouraging: "Life is God's gift to you; what you do with that life is your gift to God." Danny's life has not been without pain and struggle; however, he has overcome and has lived a successful and rewarding life and encourages us to do the same. In his book, *What Matters Most*, Danny shares the godly wisdom that can only be learned and revealed through life's experience. I believe one of Danny's primary objectives is to encourage us to make a few simple adjustments in our daily life which will help us experience a more peaceful and rewarding life.

Neal Stenzel
Chief Financial Officer, Oral Roberts University

Dedication

For Luke and Kellie, and for Rex.

Contents

Introduction

What a gift life is—possibilities and opportunities abound! Life is an adventure, and along the journey are seasons of joy and blessing and seasons of difficulty and despair. Planting and growth, pruning and death. This adventure is not for the faint of heart.

Some people, due to difficulties and loss, choose to play it safe. They take off their boots and step off the trail in a spot where they can find some reprieve from the mayhem and madness. They look for shelter from the storm and take cover. After a while, they discover they like the safety and comfort they have found and decide to reside there. They quickly adapt to their surroundings and, after a while, find that their thirst for adventure has diminished.

I hope, as you read, you will find renewal and refreshment for your journey. I hope you'll find a rekindled desire to put your boots back on, to pick up your backpack, and to continue your adventure. An end to your journey will come, but not now.

We are not always in control of our circumstances, and life rarely turns out like we imagine. I think that is a good thing; we all enjoy some element of surprise in our lives! I went to college with the idea I would major in music, yet I wasn't accepted into the program and had to find another major and, consequently, another vocation. I turned to business although, at the time, I had no particular vision for it. And so life goes.

I have been on the adventure for a while now, and there are many things I hope to do and to accomplish between now and my journey's end. For now, I offer this encouragement from the first leg of my adventure, encouragement I have been recording over several years. The following pages contain thoughts about what I've found to be the things that matter most. Why? Because our lives matter. How we live and what we do matters.

Why should my words matter to you? I'm not famous or prominent in any way, neither am I a philosopher or a theologian. I'm an ordinary person like most of you; a husband, a father, an employee, and a friend. The world needs ordinary people to live lives that matter, lives that make a difference. It isn't the experts and the thought leaders that change the world, it's the everyday people like us.

Most of life is lived in the valleys, not on the mountaintops, and most of it isn't glamorous or noteworthy. It's more like Eugene Peterson described as "a long obedience in the same direction." Trusted voices help us on our journey; voices of those who have been tested, bloodied, and scarred but have endured. Voices of those who have kept hope alive when every reason for hope seemed lost. Voices of love and compassion, friendship and forgiveness.

My hope is that you'll find my voice trustworthy and that, in these words, you'll find encouragement to live a life that matters, and ultimately, for what matters most.

CHAPTER I

Heart Matters

Guard your heart above all else, for it is the source of life.
—Proverbs 4:23 HCSB

Nothing is more important than your heart. Just as your physical heart is central to your body, so your spiritual heart is central to your inner life. When I'm referring to your spiritual heart, I am referring to the essence of who you are and the place where your motives and desires reside. And just as disease in the physical heart is a leading cause of death worldwide, so is it true that disease in the spiritual heart brings death to the core of a human being.

As you know, your physical heart is located in the center of your chest, pumping blood that carries oxygen and nutrients to the rest of your body. Your spiritual heart is located within the hidden, innermost part of you and is the center of your spiritual life. From it flows the source of life. That is why the Scriptures encourage us that, above all else we do in life, we should guard our hearts.

This idea may sound as if we're encouraged to build walls around our hearts for safety reasons. However, that is too limiting. The bigger idea is that your heart is the most important thing about you. Therefore, not only should you guard it so it doesn't become damaged or stolen, vandalized or lost, but you should tend it and keep it as you would your family or a garden, so that it can grow and flourish.

We have all heard it said that someone "lost heart." What people usually mean by this is that someone lost motivation and momentum. It could also mean that they just quit and lost the will to keep up the fight. They may continue to go through the motions, but, in reality, they have checked out and are no longer living from their heart.

What a tragedy! In contrast, we've heard of others who against all odds have kept their courage and will. I want to be counted among the latter, and I'm sure you do as well. How do we do this? How do we guard our heart so it grows healthy and strong? How do we tend the fire so that the flame doesn't die but instead burns bright, providing warmth and security in dangerous and cold surroundings?

Burning Hearts

In the Bible are many great stories of inspiration. One of my favorites is found at the end of the Gospel of Luke. In the previous two chapters, Jesus had been brutally tortured and murdered after being betrayed by one of his closest friends. The remaining disciples had fled and were now in hiding, wondering if they were next. Some women at Jesus' tomb had returned to the disciples with stories about seeing Jesus alive, saying that he had risen from the dead!

The story picks up where two of his followers were leaving the scene of the crime in Jerusalem and were walking back home to Emmaus. My guess is that all of it was too much for them. A few years before, when they first encountered Jesus, they were drawn like moths to a flame. However, recently there was so much they did not understand, and it was all so overwhelming— the brutal torture and killing, death and silence. Now there were unbelievable claims of resurrection. It was just too much, too fast. So much hope followed by so much pain. Maybe they felt like they had to protect their hearts, so they were leaving Jerusalem to create some space to figure life out again.

I can surely understand their feelings. Recently my family was ravaged with the premature death of two loved ones within a few years of each other. This was too much pain for one family in a condensed window of time. Like the disciples on the Emmaus road, I can understand how they felt too vulnerable to trust or hope again, especially so soon. So the disciples left—they left the other disciples, they left Jerusalem, they left all the chaos—and they went home.

As they were walking down the road immersed in a deep conversation, Jesus, having disguised himself as a stranger and traveler, approached them. He inquired about their discussion, and they invited him in. As they poured out their confusion and disappointment, Jesus replied, *"'How foolish you are, and how slow to believe all that the prophets have spoken! Did not the Messiah have to suffer these things and then enter his glory?' And beginning with Moses and all the Prophets, he explained to them what was said in all the Scriptures concerning himself"* (Luke 24:25-27).

As they arrived at their destination, and since it was getting late, the disciples invited Jesus to stick around and spend the evening with them. At least that's what they said; I think it was just an excuse. You see, there was something about this man, and they didn't want him to leave. Later that evening, the story unfolded:

When he was at the table with them, he took bread, gave thanks, broke it and began to give it to them. Then their eyes were opened and they recognized him, and he disappeared from their sight. They asked each other, "Were not our hearts burning within us while he talked with us on the road and opened the Scriptures to us?" They got up and returned at once to Jerusalem. There they found the Eleven and those with them, assembled together and saying, "It is true! The Lord has risen and has appeared to Simon." Then the two told what had happened on the way, and how Jesus was recognized by them when he broke the bread. (Luke 24:30-35)

I love the phrase *"were not our hearts burning within us while he talked with us on the road"* (v. 32). In the midst of the disciples' despair and confusion, broken hearts and broken dreams, Jesus once again touched them and blew on the fire of their hearts, tending the flickering flame that was there. They immediately got up from the table and, in the middle of the night, headed back to Jerusalem to let their friends know that Jesus was alive. An encounter with Jesus had changed everything.

I have found that to be true in my own life. I can be vigilant and responsible, and I can be careful and loyal; yet, even doing all of these, I, much like the disciples in the story above, can lose my way. However, as I encounter Jesus, I find a reason for living and purpose for my days. My heart comes to life and begins to burn with a zeal for him and for others. He gives me a part to play in the great story of history.

So if your heart is heavy and you feel that the flame in your heart has dimmed, if you are tired, bored or burned out, if you are a victim of trouble or trauma and your heart just can't process any more pain or disappointment, go to Jesus. He changes everything. He not only holds the answers for your troubled heart, he is the answer for your troubled heart. He created your heart, and he alone knows exactly what you need this very moment.

Capturing the Heart (Beauty)

Beauty has a way of capturing the heart like nothing else. In Oklahoma where I live, we are blessed with beautiful sunsets. I'm unsure of the conditions that make it so; however, nowhere else have I seen such hues of pink, orange, yellow, and red filling the afternoon sky as day gives way to night. For those few moments, I'm held captive by a sunset's beauty. Those moments can transform you and me, or we can quickly forget them in the rush of evening activity. To transform us, we must hold them in our heart. We enrich our lives by the beauty we behold.

I encourage you to pay attention. Don't be in such a rush that you miss the dazzling sunset filling the evening sky. Beauty comes to us regularly, but you must look at it to be changed by it. Let beauty capture your heart.

Music has always been important to me. I enjoy art in all its various forms, yet my heart is influenced by music more than any other. So I feed my soul music.

Music was so important in my early years that I wanted to be a singer. In my teens, I was involved with the music at the church my family attended. I was mentored by our music pastor, and he and his wife became my lifelong friends. She taught me piano, and he and I sang together. Music was such a big part of my life that when thinking about college, I decided to audition to be a music major. Such is the power of beauty to capture a heart!

I remember as a teen when only a song would bring the encouragement my heart needed. I have seen this in my daughter's life as well. A career in music didn't pan out for me, and that's fine. That's because beauty trumps economics, and money can't measure what matters most. Music is important to my life. It moves me and speaks to me.

Open your heart and look for beauty. Be alert to what grabs your attention. Gaze on beauty and don't worry if you can't fully grasp it, take hold of it, or understand it. That doesn't matter. As Scripture says,

> *"Whatever is lovely, whatever is admirable . . .*
> *think about such things"* (Philippians 4:8).

Stirring the Heart (Inspiration)

Our Father created this beautiful world and wants us to drink in its beauty. We all find it in different places. As the old saying goes, "Beauty is in the eyes of the beholder." Where do you find beauty, and what inspires and stirs your heart? These are important questions. Self-discovery is such an important part of life! You only have one life to live, and a big part of living is discovering who you are and how you can best live a happy, productive, and fulfilling life. Life is God's gift to you; what you do with that life is your gift to God. So in the process of discovering, part of the process is noticing what stirs your heart—keep in mind, this is not a competition with others.

One of the things that stirs my heart is friendship. Mattering to someone and making a difference in their life is important to me. Let me tell you the story of how I stumbled upon that realization.

A dear friend of mine started a ministry called Your One Degree. Its mission is to help individuals discover the purposes for which they were designed by God and to assist them in incorporating those purposes into their daily lives. As I grew in friendship with the founder, Dave Jewitt, he often asked me one of his favorite questions: "When do you feel like you've hit a home run in your life?" For the longest time that question frustrated me, as I couldn't provide an answer. One day when Dave asked the question again, I took my frustration to God and asked that he reveal to me a time when I did something significant, like hit a home run. Immediately, I thought of a recent visit with friends.

Carrie and I were in California on a short vacation built around a business trip. Before my meeting in Palm Desert, we decided to drive the Pacific Coast Highway from Los Angeles to Carmel. We had dear friends living in San Jose at the time who, when learning we would visit Carmel, set up a time for us to meet for lunch at Pebble Beach. During the visit, my friend confided that he was at a crossroads in his professional life. He was considering a major career change and asked us to listen and provide our thoughts and prayers. Over the course of the ensuing weeks, I was a sounding board, a counselor, and a friend.

As God brought that situation to mind, I immediately realized that I had encountered a home run. I mattered to a friend, and that mattered to me. As I've thought of that discovery many times since, it has helped me to realize that the most important things in life aren't measured by monetary standards. It helped me to understand that God designed me, in part, for intimacy and friendship. Although knowing this isn't particularly helpful for building a career or for gaining financially, it is important in leading a fulfilling life and living from my heart.

The journey of self-discovery really is a journey into the heart of God. The Scriptures state that God wove you together in your mother's womb. He spoke life to you, and he breathed the breath of life into your lungs. He made you for good works before the foundation of the earth. For you to know who you are is to understand more and more of your Father in heaven, and to understand how he crafted you and for what purpose. This is one of life's greatest discoveries. In fact, I believe the great adventure of our lives is to explore the height, width, breadth, and depth of God in the world and in ourselves. Our own lives are the reflection of his nature. We have embarked on a never-ending adventure, and we may never fully uncover the full mystery, even throughout eternity. Such, I believe, is the magnitude of the inspiration of God.

As you learn and discover what inspires you, I encourage you to do more and more of it. Feed the fire! Tend to your heart and ensure it stays nurtured; well fed and well watered. Learn to ensure your heart stays healthy and strong, filled with inspiration. The journey is long and arduous, and I assure you, you will need every ounce of inspiration you can find.

Overwhelming the Heart (Wonder)

Over a decade ago, I was feeling stuck and quite discouraged. One of my dearest friends offered to fly me to his home in Oregon for a break from my routine. I accepted his invitation and flew to Portland. We visited with his family for a day, then drove to the Oregon Coast for the weekend.

Pete and I have enjoyed a rich friendship spanning over three decades. We don't have to do much to entertain ourselves, we just enjoy each other's company. We each have a passion for our shared faith, and we both value friendships.

I remember many details of the weekend: walking the beautiful Oregon beach, feeling the ocean spray and the cold Pacific water, and driving up and down the coastline on high ridges overlooking the rough winter waters. One sunny afternoon, I remember stopping at a lookout hundreds of feet above the water below and watching coast guard boats practice rescue operations in the thrashing surf. I remember Pete and I talking late into the night about things we valued: our families, our faith, and our work. We talked about Rich Mullins who had recently died, and we talked about simplicity and trust.

But the thing I remember most about the weekend is breathing. I remember exhaling, and I remember sighing. I remember inhaling long, slow breaths, holding my breath, and slowly exhaling.

Why would I remember such a thing? I was tired, and I was discouraged. I wasn't carrying much hope of things changing. Life was weighing heavy on me, and I needed hope. Slowing down, enjoying the moment, and being in the presence of a dear friend began the restoration of hope in me. It is the simplest of things that can cause wonder to grow.

I hope you wonder. I hope you wonder every day. Even as I'm writing this, I am looking out my window on a late-fall morning as the last vestiges of foliage gleam brightly in the sun. The leaves, the sun, the seasons; all reasons to celebrate and wonder.

However, if we aren't careful, the demands and responsibilities that life brings can consume us. Before long, we lose our sense of wonder. These demands come from good places. They come from places like our families; families into which we're born and later into which we build through marriage. They come from our jobs; places in which we labor to contribute to society and to build a better world for ourselves, our families, our communities, and nations. They come from our education, where we seek to grow in understanding of the world in which we live. They come from our shared communities and places of worship where we invest ourselves for our faith, friends, and families because of our deepest convictions.

These demands and responsibilities are important, and in no way do I want to minimize them. Nevertheless, don't lose your wonder. Children wonder easily; getting lost in moments of pleasure and activity, forgetting the world around them. Maybe that's why we consider wonder as childlikeness.

A child in wonder is beautiful, but not an adult who chases daydreams and fantasies. We have other words for them, and they aren't flattering. Still, we need wonder. We need moments to be arrested by beauty, calmed by simplicity, or stirred by nobility and courage.

Life is bigger than you and me. It offers more knowledge and beauty than we can ever behold within our short lives. So let's embrace as much as we can! Let's strive to be forever curious, ever learning, ever marveling at the mysteries in the universe. Let's wonder at the beauty around us and take time to celebrate while we live purposefully, responsibly, and intentionally each day. Let's keep our hearts open to the wonder of love that is as near as our own family and our own hearts.

Greater than Our Hearts (Glory)

A passage in the book of Acts states that when people saw the boldness and courage of the disciples, it was evident they had been with Jesus. The disciples were so remarkably different that the only way others could describe the difference was that they had been with Jesus. The Old Testament presence of God was referred to as his glory. This glory was typically accompanied by a great light; a light so bright, it was difficult to look at. This light is what Saul encountered on the road to Damascus when he encountered Jesus. The same light was seen on the Mount of Transfiguration and also on Mount Sinai.

When Moses met with God, the Bible says his face would actually glow and radiate the light of God's glory because of his time spent with the Lord. I desire my life to be that same way. I want my life with God to be evident to all around me, so people know I've been with Jesus and have spent time in his presence.

Moses wasn't a superman. He didn't become holier and holier; he just chose to be God's friend. I also want to be God's friend, dwelling in his presence and spending time with him. I want to be transformed by his presence like the disciples on the road to Emmaus. Just as time in the sun tans us, time in God's presence transforms us. It doesn't come as much from our efforts and energies as much as it comes from being in his presence. Yes, God is greater than our hearts, but our hearts were made for his glory.

CHAPTER 2

Prayer Matters

I wasn't in the room with Dad when he passed. For years he had been suffering with Parkinson's disease and dementia. During the months preceding his death, he had grown weaker and was unable to eat. At the end, Mom was unable to care for him on her own. His last fifteen days were spent at Clarehouse, a beautiful hospice home in Tulsa.

I was mowing the grass when I got the news. I got to Clarehouse as fast as I could and entered the room to hear Mom crying like I had never heard her before. It was a deep, painful wailing from a place I had never encountered. Dad's body was lying on the bed in front of me, but I knew he was no longer there. The realization that he had been alive just moments before but now was alive to a different reality was so real to me, it was palpable. The physical and spiritual worlds seemed to collide, and the separation between the two seemed indistinguishable. I have heard these referred to as "thin places," places where the separation of our earthly lives from God's presence seems small. I knew Dad was alive, just not where I could see or touch him. How could he be far away, since he had just been breathing the same air I was now?

For years I had grieved the loss of my dad as I had known him. In these first moments after his passing, I felt more peace than I had in quite some time. The reality of eternity and its nearness brought great comfort.

I was forty-one at the time, in the middle of both my career and parenting years. Now all striving for success in my personal and professional life seemed inconsequential. It wasn't that accomplishments were unimportant, yet the striving to be all that I could be and the pressure that came with doing my best in every area had taken its toll. Surely that was not the abundant life Jesus had promised!

In those moments, as I grieved the loss of my dad, I felt peace; peace that everything was okay and that all things work together for good. A peace that God's plan for me would come to pass, and I would not miss it. A peace that his plans are not just for the small amount of time that we spend on earth but will last throughout eternity. A peace that life's journey does not end in death but continues forever. I cannot overstate the impact these thoughts made on my heart. I am thankful for thin places.

Mystery

My dad's parting gift to me was the reminder of the importance of eternity and its nearness, so important yet so mysterious. So is prayer. I love the idea of prayer, but often I get tripped up in its practice. Prayer is like so many other areas of life where I disqualify myself due to feelings of inadequacy. And the longer I live, the more I realize how little I know and understand about most things, and this certainly applies to prayer.

Mike Yaconelli wrote this same confession in his profound book *Messy Spirituality.* Upon hearing Mike declare himself a failure at prayer, a dear friend bristled at the thought and offered a fresh perspective. Knowing Mike well and his heart for God, she encouraged him to see that every thought turned toward God is prayer. Eyes need not be closed, nor knees bowed. Every time God's name is called, no matter how brief, is prayer.

That idea encourages me greatly because I, too, feel like a prayer failure, though I do love God deeply and think about him often. Maybe I'm better at prayer than I initially thought. A pastor friend of mine once described prayer as unbroken intimacy with God. I love that definition, as my heart longs for intimacy and communion with God. Even so, many times in my pursuit of that intimacy, I am left longing for something more.

Invitation

One thing is for certain: God invites us to come close, to draw near. Throughout all of Scripture, from Genesis to Revelation, this invitation is repeatedly offered. Prayer is our response to that invitation. And once we respond, God astonishes us with his care, going so far as to ask such personal questions as, "What do you want?" and "What can I do for you?"

Periodically I go to a place a few hours from home to clear my head, to seek solitude, and to be alone with God. It's a one-room cabin in the woods behind a little country church. Near the cabin is a small trail, about a mile long, that follows the top of a hill bordered by ravines and dense trees. Along the path appear wooden signs engraved with scripture verses. I have frequented this spot many times through the years and, every time, I'm overwhelmed by the invitation of God memorialized in the wood.

Come on a brief walk with me on top of the hill—a prayerful walk. Step out of the cabin and turn right where the path is rocky and worn, yet small flowers and clover push up through the dirt. After about twenty yards, we find the first sign and read: *"Call to Me, and I will answer and show you great and unsearchable things you do not know"* (BSB).

Underneath the verse is a reference where it is found. This one happens to be Jeremiah 33:3, which is special to me because it is my favorite scripture verse and thirty-three is my favorite number. But more important is God's promise that if we call, he will answer. In addition, he promises to show us great things and unsearchable things, things currently unknown. What a promise!

For the remainder of this path, I'll let you walk alone with God. I encourage you not to rush, but to slowly walk between each sign and linger on the words. You might even stop to meditate on what you find:

"This is the confidence which we have before Him, that, if we ask anything according to His will, He hears us. And if we know that He hears us in whatever we ask, we know that we have the requests which we have asked from Him" (1 John 5:14,15 NASB).

"If you abide in me, and my words abide in you, ask whatever you wish, and it will be done for you" (John 15:7 ESV).

"Again I say to you, that if two of you agree on earth about anything that they may ask, it shall be done for them by My Father who is in heaven" (Matthew 18:19 NASB).

"Whatever you ask in my name, this I will do, that the Father may be glorified in the Son. If you ask me anything in my name, I will do it" (John 14:13-14 ESV).

"Delight yourself also in the Lord, and He shall give you the desires of your heart. Commit your way to the Lord, trust also in Him, and He shall bring it to pass" (Psalm 37:4,5 NKJV).

I hope your heart is stirred and you are moved by God's invitations. There are hundreds more. Invitations like . . .

"Come, all you who are thirsty, come to the waters; and you who have no money, come, buy and eat! Come, buy wine and milk without money and without cost" (Isaiah 55:1).

"I am the bread of life. Whoever comes to me will never go hungry, and whoever believes in me will never be thirsty" (John 6:35).

"Let anyone who is thirsty come to me and drink" (John 7:37).

If you're feeling lost and hopeless about how to respond to the invitation of God, don't be discouraged. Instead, just come to Jesus as simply as you can. This isn't a performance but a response. About our response, I've heard the following attributed to Søren Kierkegaard, a famous Danish theologian, philosopher, and poet: "Jesus says, 'Come!' But if, alas, one is in such distress he cannot come, a sigh is enough: to long for him is to come to him."

Response

My feelings of inadequacy have been one obstacle to pursuing faithfulness in prayer. Another is attempts at prayer that don't resonate with my heart. Having grown up in church, I've been in many prayer meetings and involved with thousands of prayers. Many of those have seemed heartfelt and authentic, others contrived and hollow. Some have grated on me and left me wanting to run. It's a poor excuse, but true nonetheless, that I have allowed those feeble attempts to hinder an authentic life of prayer of my own.

For whatever prayer is or isn't, looking to Jesus is helpful for understanding how to respond to God's invitation. If we know anything about Jesus, we know that he prayed. He prayed all the time. He got up early, and he stayed out late. He went to the wilderness, and he went to the mountain. He found a quiet spot on the hillside, and he found a favorite spot in a garden. The Scripture states that he *"often withdrew to deserted places and prayed"* (Luke 5:16 HCSB). This was not an isolated incident but his custom and practice.

So my first encouragement to you in responding to his invitation is to find a quiet place to pray, then pray. Find a spot you like and just be with him.

I have a few such spots. The first is in my living room in the early-morning hours before anyone else is awake. My custom is to brew a cup of coffee and to find a comfortable spot on my couch and to be with God for the first moments of my day.

Another spot is a cemetery near my office that I frequent during lunch breaks. It is a quiet place without traffic, so finding solitude is easy. Many times I walk among the tombstones reflecting on the lives lived and their purposes, and mine. I have many entries in my journal of the thoughts God has shared with me during our times together there.

Carrie and I like to take walks in the late afternoon and, many times, these walks evolve into times of prayer. I have friends who spend early-morning walks with God. Be creative and find places where you can withdraw and allow your heart to open.

Simple

Next, I encourage you to keep it simple. I've heard it said that "the heart can receive no more than the seat can endure." If you grew up in a Christian home, I'm sure you endured times of prayer that seemed like they would never end. Many church services seem to be the same way, and there are times and places for that. Many times Jesus prayed all night or late into the evening hours. And when times were toughest, Jesus leaned into prayer even more.

Yet, for normal, day-to-day life, I encourage you to keep it simple. Let your prayers be simple, authentic thoughts and offerings from your heart to God. The most clear and helpful instruction from Jesus on prayer is found in Matthew 6. Basically, he says to keep it short and sweet:

> *"Whenever you pray, you must not be like the hypocrites, because they love to pray standing in the synagogues and on the street corners to be seen by people. I assure you: They've got their reward! But when you pray, go into your private room, shut your door, and pray to your Father who is in secret. And your Father who sees in secret will reward you. When you pray, don't babble like the idolaters, since they imagine they'll be heard for their many words. Don't be like them, because your Father knows the things you need before you ask Him"*
> (Matthew 6:5-8 HCSB).

In the verses that follow, Jesus gives us an example of how to pray. Some say it's a model prayer, and most know it as the Lord's Prayer. The Gospel of Luke says that after Jesus had finished praying in a certain place, one of his disciples asked him to teach the disciples to pray. Jesus began by saying, *"Whenever you pray, say this"* (Luke 11:2 HCSB). This is the same prayer found in Matthew 6 where Jesus says, *"You should pray like this"* (Matthew 6:9 HCSB).

"Our Father which art in heaven, Hallowed be thy name.
Thy kingdom come, Thy will be done in earth, as it is in heaven.
Give us this day our daily bread. And forgive us our debts,
as we forgive our debtors. And lead us not into temptation,
but deliver us from evil: For thine is the kingdom, and the power,
and the glory, for ever. Amen" (Matthew 6:9-13 KJV).

Be Still and Know

Recently I saw the movie *Risen* which follows the journey of Clavius, a Roman tribune tasked with finding the body of a crucified Jew named Jesus. Jewish leaders wanted his body located to disprove rumors that he rose from the dead. Clavius had seen Jesus die on the cross and had sealed his tomb. While looking for the body, he instead encounters the risen Christ. He then follows Jesus from Jerusalem to Galilee, overwhelmed with wonder while trying to grasp what he is encountering.

While sleeping under the open sky, he awakes to find Jesus sitting alone. His mind still racing from everything he can't understand, he approaches Jesus and takes a seat on the ground near him. While enjoying the calm and the stars, very little is said. It was a "be still and know" kind of moment.

If we are not careful, we can misguidedly make our journey about ourselves and what we do. I encourage you to keep the emphasis on Jesus. Be with him, and be still. Quiet your mind and heart. When I saw Clavius arise to be with Jesus, something stirred within. I also wanted to be with Jesus.

I like to be productive. I like to achieve and accomplish. I keep lists and a planner filled with things to do. I also like to journal and keep track of what I've done. I even keep a bucket list of the really big things I would like to do before I die. The problem with lists is there are always more items on them than can possibly get done. Therefore, on most days, I feel like I haven't done enough. Another byproduct is living distracted in the current moment because I'm thinking about the many moments ahead. This mindset is in contrast to the idea of being still.

As I'm writing this, it's a Saturday. I awoke today and, as normal, spent time in God's Word. After coffee and breakfast, my mind started pursuing my list of all the things to do. I became discouraged as my list was longer than my day. But on this day, I sat down, closed my eyes, and was still.

I'm not sure how being still works, but it does. A scripture verse that gives definition and color to the phenomenon that happens when we're still, making space for God, is *"in quietness and trust is your strength"* (Isaiah 30:15). Another is *"those who wait for the Lord shall renew their strength, they shall mount up with wings like eagles, they shall run and not be weary, they shall walk and not faint"* (Isaiah 40:31 NRSV). I usually think of building strength through working out, not through stillness and waiting, but waiting worked for me again today.

I don't know how long I sat quietly in my chair without saying a word or uttering a prayer. However, as I sat, I felt the peaceful presence of the Lord. And during those moments, he gave me both peace and strength for the day.

Unique

Know that you are unique. God will speak and interact with you differently than he interacts with me. Trust that he knows how to get through to you. You can't have my experience; God has something special, tailor-made for you. He has words for you, purposes for you, people for you, and desires for you.

Don't force it, and don't fake it. Continue to ask, seek, and knock. Then wait, look, and listen. Hear what he may say, and see what he may do. Whatever it is, however small it seems, embrace it, celebrate it, and see what he may do with it.

Help

Years ago when I was feeling stuck, I had a good job and a wonderful family, but I couldn't see the future clearly. When I considered my station in life, a recurrent image came to mind. The image was of a small wooden rowboat in the middle of a vast ocean. The boat had no oars and no sail, and when I scanned the horizon in any direction, all I saw was water. I longed to move but had no idea which direction to go. It became clear that if I was going to be saved, it wasn't going to be from self-effort—I needed help!

The longer I live, the more I realize that life is more about him and less about me. I don't have the direction and answers for my life. Therefore, the more I exchange my plans for his, the better I am. Psalm 127:1 declares, *"Unless the Lord builds the house, the builders labor in vain."* I don't want to labor in vain and waste this gift of life. I want to trust his leading and follow his direction. He is the Good Shepherd, and I trust him to lead me to green pastures and still waters. When I find myself in dark valleys or horizonless seas, I can pray and trust him to lead me.

CHAPTER 3

Humility Matters

Whatever we have—whatever talents and abilities, our looks, our predispositions to kindness and charity, our drives and motivations—all of these are gifts from God. Some may seem like blessings and others like curses. Whatever they are, they didn't originate in us. They were given to us by our heavenly Father.

In omnipotence and greatness, he wove us together inside of our mothers' wombs. He chose the times and places where we would be born and the families into which he would place us. Since this is true, I encourage you to embrace humility as the proper perspective for our lives. God is greater, and we are lesser. He is the creator, and we are the created. He is the father, and we are the children. No matter how clearly you see or understand, it will always fall short, as God is always greater.

God is not only greater but better than you think. I love the verse in Romans where Paul asks the question, "What can separate us from this great love?" His answer is absolutely nothing can (see Romans 8:35-39). God's love is greater than we can imagine.

Though humble and small compared to his greatness, we aren't insignificant. On the contrary, we are God's children and therefore heirs to the kingdom of heaven. But this great King is unlike any we've ever known or imagined. Though his glory is great, he is humble. Of the many mysteries in life, this is one of them!

Good Pride versus Bad Pride

Most of us understand humility without having to resort to a dictionary. Simplistically, it is the opposite of arrogance or pride. Other definitions include having a modest opinion of yourself or not thinking you're better than others.

Before we throw the word *pride* under the bus completely, let's take a moment to fully consider its meaning. Pride is one of those interesting words that can have two very different meanings. On one hand it can be a vice, and on another a virtue. In other words, there can be both a good and bad pride.

We all know what bad pride looks like. It includes conceit and an inflated view of oneself. This pride should be rightly condemned. Good pride, on the other hand, represents the very best part of something. I have pride in my family's legacy; the honor, integrity, and humility with which my parents lived their lives. I also have pride in my heavenly Father and the nature and character found in his kingdom. Good pride can also be reflected in a healthy honor and respect, even for oneself.

Good pride can be displayed in the satisfaction derived from accomplishments or in strength of character. We have heard a valiant person described as having mettle. It also includes fortitude and resolve, grit and bravery. Pride encompasses all of these and can be a tremendous force for good. It can be useful for setting and maintaining high standards and can be a unifying force, able to lift and encourage.

Pride can be glorious, like the splendor of civilizations past. It is good when it stays within proper boundaries. Yet, outside of these, it comes before a fall.

Heroes of Humility

In any endeavor, it helps to have examples to follow. In the pursuit of humility, the list of examples is shorter than in most other endeavors.

However, there are names and there are stories that we can look to for inspiration.

The list includes names such as Jackie Robinson, Rosa Parks, Martin Luther King Jr., and Nelson Mandela. These endured great humiliation and persecution while they stood for equal rights. The list includes Mother Teresa who chose a life of labor among the dying and destitute in Calcutta instead of other choices she could have made. Abraham Lincoln is surely on the list.

I don't know a tremendous amount about these individuals other than what I have seen on television, in film, or in print. Others I know more intimately, through a deeper study or a more personal encounter. These have set a high bar for me personally, and I would like to introduce them to you. They are some of my heroes of humility, though I'm sure they would hate that title.

Dad

The first one is my dad. My dad's full name was James Donald Kittinger, and he went by the name of Don. He was quiet and unassuming, much like the small Kentucky town of Owensboro where he was born and raised. Dad was bright; not only did he graduate at the top of his class from the University of Kentucky, but he married my mom.

Dad was in the ROTC and, upon graduation, began his career as an officer in the United States Air Force. The one passion of his life next to his love for Mom was his love of flying. He would rather fly than do just about anything else, and flying is what he loved about his job.

Dad was a man of few words. It wasn't that he wouldn't talk; he just didn't talk much, particularly about himself. After graduating from college, I realized I didn't know much about his Vietnam experience where he had flown over 240 missions. When I was home one summer, Dad and I were driving from our home in Mississippi to a friend's lake home in Alabama. We had a few hours' drive ahead of us, so I asked him to share some memories of the war. The only story he told was a self-deprecating one. He shared how, in bombing a supply line, he almost blew his plane out of the sky. That was Dad. Instead of telling me any successes, he told me of his failure.

Dad was also a kind man and a hard worker. He took care of things entrusted to him without fuss or fanfare. He was a good man and lived with integrity. He would never cut corners or cheat.

When he retired from the air force, he looked for a flying job. However, the pastor of our church, whom we affectionately called Brother B, had other plans. My family was extremely involved in our local church, and my parents were dearly loved there—so much so that Brother B didn't want to lose them to another job or city. So, he offered my dad a job as an associate pastor. At first, Dad could not imagine going from fighter pilot to pastor and had no interest in the job. He was offered a few flying jobs, none of which he felt good about taking. After much prayer and consideration, Dad accepted the associate pastor job. This was an act of humility on his part. Never in a million years did he believe he was the right fit for that job, and never in a billion years did he think he would continue working in that church for over twenty years!

Dad handled many responsibilities at Cedar Lake. As the job unfolded, his main responsibility and the one that endeared him to the congregation was his role as minister of pastoral care. What is a minister of pastoral care? I'm not sure what it is elsewhere, but what it looked like for Dad was driving our Volkswagen bus around Biloxi, picking up members too feeble to drive themselves to church, week after week, year after year.

It also included my parents making phone calls to visitors, greeting them and making them feel welcome. Mom and Dad also offered themselves for home visits to answer questions about the church community or about what it meant to be a follower of Christ. And finally, if anyone in the church was sick or hospitalized, my parents would be by their side offering friendship and comfort.

They wanted folks at Cedar Lake to know they weren't alone. They wanted them to know they were loved by God. My parents believed the best way to show that love was to be there. They spent countless hours and countless miles driving up and down the Gulf Coast to homes and hospitals. They spent countless hours drinking coffee in living rooms and waiting rooms, just being with people. On multiple occasions they drove for days across state lines to sit with families while loved ones underwent surgery.

My dad never felt gifted at this job or believed he was doing anything extraordinary. He was just being himself. Dad was humble and is my first hero of humility.

Mom

Everything I have described of Dad I equally attribute to Mom. She was Dad's better half and always by his side. My parents were best friends and partners and a shining example of a successful marriage.

I never heard one criticize the other. When the church hired Dad, they got two for the price of one, as Mom was with Dad in most everything he did. And though she was unpaid, and he was paid a modest salary, they gave it their all.

Carrie

Growing up I was fortunate to have Mom and Dad as heroes of humility in my home. Equally, in my marriage I have found another. My wife is the finest human being I have ever known. Her love and concern for others, her love for God, and her desire to always do the right thing make her shine like a star.

I can't remember a time when Carrie was mean-spirited to anyone. I have no recollection of her ever having demonstrated indifference or lack of care when a need was presented. She will stop whatever she is doing to help others. At social gatherings, she wants to ensure everyone is loved and affirmed. She is an encourager with a kind word for all. She is a servant. She does not carry offense.

I believe some people look at Carrie with her wonderful attributes and think life is easy for her, and so they judge it easy for her to be gracious, loving, and kind. However, the truth is that Carrie has learned the secret of humility. She's respected and loved because she takes a low seat and goes above and beyond in service to others. She serves when no one is watching, without pay, reward, or motivation other than to care for others and to put their needs above her own.

Carrie has served the churches that we have called home in more capacities that I can enumerate here. Some may see and envy the positions she holds. Yet, the roads to whatever positions or places she has held have been paved by serving.

One example where she has faithfully served is the position of women's Bible study leader. For some, the position looks admirable due to the leadership required. In reality, the position entails hours of calls and emails. It includes arriving first, ensuring the room is prepared. It includes greeting women, helping them feel honored and loved. It includes refreshment coordination and preparation. It includes ensuring lessons are prepared, leaders understand their roles, and that something valuable is imparted to the attendees. It looks like service.

Carrie's life hasn't been easy, as most lives aren't. We all are confronted with some level of brokenness. The details of Carrie's story are hers to tell. However, I will tell you that she has been overlooked and underappreciated and that she has served without thanks and without notice. She has even been forgotten. Such is our common road. However, in her pain and brokenness, and more important, in her love and humility, she has continued to offer herself to others. Like I said, she is the finest human being I have ever met, and I am so grateful for her!

Joseph

In addition to these three, the Scriptures provide us with many other heroes of humility to consider. I would like to describe a few that have captured my attention. First there is Joseph, the favored son of Jacob. Joseph was a dreamer with big plans. His father didn't help the situation by so highly favoring him above his brothers that they considered murdering him. The brothers eventually faked his death, lied about it, and sold him into slavery. Joseph learned one lesson after another about disappointment and betrayal. As a slave and prisoner in a foreign country, he became a broken and humble man. From the despondency of a prison cell, he rose to a staggering position of prominence. The lessons of his broken life paved the way for him to offer himself in humble service to Egypt and eventually to his family from Israel—so much so that he saved both nations from famine and brought them untold wealth.

Moses

Then there is Moses, the adopted son of Pharaoh who fell from grace upon murdering a fellow Egyptian. After fleeing to the desert and living the humble life of a shepherd for forty years, God invited him into a great deliverance plan for his people in Egypt. Moses decried his qualifications and abilities, yet God's persistence prevailed. Because of Moses' humility, God was able to do mighty things through a broken and willing friend.

David

Next is a shepherd boy named David, the youngest of his father's sons. When asked by the prophet Samuel about his sons, David's father failed to mention him. Even so, God had big plans for David who became a national hero when he faced and killed Goliath in the Valley of Elah.

After that tremendous victory, King Saul brought David into his home with a jealous eye and a heart to kill. During the next thirteen years, Saul sought opportunity after opportunity to kill this heroic young man while

David spent those years on the run, living in caves and under the open sky, always looking over his shoulder and fearing for his life. These difficulties and persecutions were the tools God used to prepare David to live a life as Israel's greatest king. David had survived humility training 101.

Jesus

Finally, the list would be incomplete without the greatest hero of humility: Jesus. Though God himself, Jesus was born to a young virgin in a poor village in Galilee. And this happened in tiny Israel while under the occupation of the powerful Roman army during a time of great civil unrest.

For thirty years he lived in obscurity in the tiny backwater town of Nazareth. At the appointed time, he began to roam the countryside proclaiming the nearness of the kingdom of God. While proclaiming good news, he served and he loved, healing some from their infirmities and delivering others from demonic oppression. He touched the untouchable, loved the unlovable, and embraced the outcasts, prostitutes, drunks, and even the hated Romans.

In his humility, he reached out to all. The world had never seen anything like him; yet after three years of public ministry, he was publicly betrayed and murdered at the young age of thirty-three. On the evening of his betrayal, he did something extraordinary: he demonstrated his humility by taking the role of a servant. That night he not only washed the feet of his friends but also those of his betrayer. He then instructed his followers to do likewise; to love and to serve one another.

Do Likewise

Life has a way of humbling us. This is not through choice but is simply a part of our shared experience. Our stories and circumstances, though vastly different, all carry this common thread. For some, it may be a failure of some sort, whether on the job, in the family or home, or in finances or faith. For others it may be a crushing blow in health. Others may be stung by betrayal of a friend or spouse, while others are assaulted by unkind and demeaning words.

My dad, midway through his air force career, endured the repeated humiliation of his superiors overlooking him for promotion. There is a longer story here, but the short version is that one particular man ensured that Dad would never rise far in rank. It was cruel and unfair, and all other officers for whom Dad worked argued for his promotion. Even then, they couldn't undo what this demeaning officer had done.

My wife was betrayed by a previous fiancé. While Carrie traveled on a mission trip before her senior year in college, her fiancé pursued a relationship with another woman. Carrie returned to campus excited to see her love, but instead found humiliation and a broken heart.

I have been humiliated on numerous occasions. I have been ridiculed for how I look, for what I said or how I said it. And while humiliations come regularly through endless sources, how we respond determines the weight of our character. While we admire the great ones among us who walk in humility, we despise the humiliation endured that led to its formation.

Those who endure and embrace humility shine brightly. They arise from dust and ashes and walk in strength and newness of life. They neither drown in sorrow nor are they filled with bitterness from the injustice endured.

Tools for Humility

Author Rick Warren wrote, "Humility is not thinking less of yourself; it's thinking of yourself less." You become what you think about. If you choose to dwell on the past, its humiliations and injustice, it will be difficult to move into the future that awaits you. The world is enriched by those who allow the furnace of difficulty and humiliation to burn away the dross of pride and selfishness with which we all wrestle. To allow the difficulty to have its way is to nurture the soil from which greatness can be born.

The brother of Jesus wrote as much when he penned the following words:

> *"Consider it pure joy, my brothers and sisters, whenever you face trials of many kinds, because you know that the testing of your faith produces perseverance. Let perseverance finish its work so that you may be mature and complete, not lacking anything. . . . Believers in humble circumstances ought to take pride in their high position. . . . Blessed is the one who perseveres under trial because, having stood the test, that person will receive the crown of life that the Lord has promised to those who love him"* (James 1:2-4, 9, 12).

We don't get to choose what happens to us, but we do get to choose our response. Herein lies our ultimate power and our greatest tool for victorious living. The power of choice allows us to live in the present with an eye toward the future, rather than to stay mired in the past. Instead of embracing bitterness or a whole host of other things like jealousy, rage, and addiction, we choose good, we choose hope, and we choose humility. We entrust ourselves to God, placing our lives into his capable hands.

Another tool to use in our pursuit of humility is the example of our heroes who model how to live and rise above difficulty and injustice. Finally, we have the very words of God reminding us of the importance of humility, though his encouragement flies in the face of our natural inclinations. Such encouragements include these:

- *"It is the one who is least among you all who is the greatest"* (Luke 9:48).
- *"The last will be first, and the first will be last"* (Matthew 20:16).
- *"Do nothing from selfish ambition or conceit, but in humility count others more significant than yourselves. Let each of you look not only to his own interests, but also to the interests of others"* (Philippians 2:3-4 ESV).

- *"The greatest among you shall be your servant. Whoever exalts himself will be humbled, and whoever humbles himself will be exalted"* (Matthew 23:11-12 ESV).

- *"Whoever humbles himself like this child is the greatest in the kingdom of heaven"* (Matthew 18:4 ESV).

- *"You, my brothers and sisters, were called to be free. But do not use your freedom to indulge the flesh; rather, serve one another humbly in love"* (Galatians 5:13).

The path is difficult; walking in humility is not easy. It is the road less traveled. Robert Frost wrote so beautifully,

> Two roads diverged in a wood, and I—
> I took the one less traveled by,
> And that has made all the difference.
> ("The Road Not Taken")

Our nature is to vie for ourselves, to fight for position and promotion. Fighting for ourselves is a part of life. So is self-care and self-love. Yet, God knew we needed to be reminded of the importance of others, so he instructed us to love and to care for others with the same level of love and care we offer to ourselves. The strongest and best among us are those who selflessly serve their fellow man, who live not for self-gain and self-promotion but for the betterment of others. May you be one who has the courage, strength, and dignity to choose to live in humility.

CHAPTER 4

Hope Matters

We all have hopes and dreams. I'm not sure where they come from, but we have them nonetheless. I am suspicious that our heavenly Father imparted them into our hearts as he knit us together in our mothers' wombs. Maybe we received them the moment he breathed his life into our lungs. Or, knowing the families and communities in which we would belong and where we would grow, maybe he knew our hopes and dreams would be born along the way. Maybe he knew that, in those places, hope would be sown, watered, and nurtured. No matter where they began, my heart cries out with the psalmist for you, *"May he give you the desire of your heart and make all your plans succeed"* (Psalm 20:4).

Hope Defined

Merriam-Webster's defines "hope" this way: "to cherish a desire with anticipation." Hope carries with it a longing and expectancy for something desired. I long and desire for many things, so I guess I'm filled with hope. But, like you, many of my hopes have gone unmet. Even worse were those that were crushed, leaving me brokenhearted and disappointed. I have also felt the heartsickness described in Proverbs due to deferred hope (see Proverbs 13:12).

Persevere in Hope

Through all the delays and disappointments, we must persevere in hope. Hope is crucial to our survival and success. If we become depleted of hope or lose hope, life becomes colorless and tasteless. Hope provides the spark for our days and the strength we need to shoulder the burdens that come as we move toward our desires.

As long as your heart has hope, you have the ability to endure great difficulty, to continue through endless monotony, to scale heights, and to plumb depths. Without it, all becomes lost. Some live without hope, but that isn't the life I want to live.

I've had many disappointments in my life. I've been disappointed in relationships and disappointed by the weather. I have been disappointed by pay raises, by elections, and by the scores of football games. Disappointments are a normal part of life. They are as normal as breathing. They come at all of us indiscriminately. We shouldn't fear them or shrink back from fully living because of them. Instead, our choices made in their midst affect the quality of life we live.

As disappointments come, we hold the ultimate power of life—the power of choice. Viktor Frankl, the noted Austrian physician and Holocaust survivor, described this power in his book *Man's Search for Meaning*. To paraphrase, he wrote that between stimulus and response, each holds the power to choose. How we respond to disappointments makes all the difference in our lives.

During my senior year of college, my scuba class spent spring break in the Florida Keys for a week of scuba diving. We dove one day, but the rest was cancelled due to a storm system that settled over southern Florida for the week. This was not the week our scuba class had hoped for. Still, I have some really great memories from that trip. Looking for things to do, a friend and I found an old sailboat underneath the home where we were staying. I had never sailed, but Mark had. We decided to take that old Sunfish out in the Atlantic despite the rough seas and gusty winds, and we had a ball! Halfway into our voyage, the wind ripped our sail—the possibility of another disappointment! In actuality, the adventure became more exciting: Mark steered the boat while I became part of the sail, and somehow, we made it back to shore. Mark and I have multiple scuba experiences to remember, but very few ripped-sail, stormy-sea sailboat excursions. It's a fond memory.

In recent years I was invited to go diving again. It had been over twenty-five years since my last excursion, so I took a refresher class, saved up a little money, and joined my friends Steve and Matt for a trip to Santa Catalina, Panama. From there we took an hour-long boat ride each day to Coiba, where the water is deep, cold, and filled with sharks. Oh, and by the way, it rained the entire time we were there. The boat was mostly uncovered and, although we wore wet suits, we were cold and wet the entire ride to and from our accommodations. In addition, on one of our deepest dives, my mask leaked the entire time.

Yet, it was a trip of a lifetime! We commented during our stay that our wives would have hated it. However, we felt like our man-cards had been punched. We had encountered difficult circumstances and disappointments, but, through it all, we had an amazing scuba adventure. We encountered a giant grouper that was over seven feet long, we dove with sharks on every dive, we swam near a school of a thousand barracuda, and we encountered manta rays, turtles, and moray eels. It was amazing!

We all walk through disappointing circumstances, some small and others large. For many, the temptation is to stop and to stay there, embracing the disappointment. It's not that it's a pleasant place to stay; it's just that those who do so may have encountered more than life's fair share of trouble and are so battered and bruised that hope seems like the more painful alternative. The reality of their experience has communicated that disappointment and despair are a greater reality than hope. They hunker down and endure, rather than press ahead and continue to hope for a better day.

As I look back on many of life's disappointments, I can now see good. Enduring difficulty and heartbreak is sweetened by redemption. It doesn't mean that the heartbreak or disappointment was good in and of itself. It just means that they were not the end of the story. The apostle Paul wrote it this way: *"And we know that in all things God works for the good of those who love him, who have been called according to his purpose"* (Romans 8:28). It isn't that all things are good, but that God works in all things for our good.

I want to encourage you with the adage, "If you're going through hell, keep going." Don't stop there, and surely, don't quit. We must never give up on hope. We must cling to the vision of a brighter future and a better tomorrow.

Work on Hope

I have found it to be true that we must work toward what we hope for and take steps in the direction of our dreams, no matter how tiny or insignificant those steps may seem. If I want to build a financial future for my family, I should find gainful employment and work hard, then save and invest wisely. If I want deep friendships, I must first be a friend and give myself to friendship. If I want to be a good father, I must be available and present to my children. If I want a fruitful marriage, I must live in such a way that reflects that desire and hope.

I can desire and hope for these things all day long, but if I don't move in their direction, it's highly unlikely they will come to fruition. Conversely, if I act on them, even though I may never fully receive all that I hope and dream for, chances are I will receive more and more of what I desire. I've heard it said that it's much easier to move a boulder once it's rolling downhill than when it's sitting still. The same is true for our hopes and dreams: we may not know all that we desire and hope for, but as we act on what we know, it will be easier to make course corrections.

If we stay stuck in hopelessness and despair, we'll live far below the abundant life God has in mind for us. We shouldn't expect much to change on its own, as if the winds of fortune will suddenly change our circumstances. I'm not denying the existence of times and seasons; what

I'm saying is that God has given us the ability to choose and to act on our hopes and dreams. Should we not do our part, we should not expect much to change. The brilliant Albert Einstein is attributed with saying, "The definition of insanity is doing the same thing over and over again but expecting different results."

Fight for Hope

Life has a way of rocking us to the core. Hopeless circumstances come and strip off the veneer of our outward life down to our base. This is the core of who we are, and it contains what we truly believe about life, ourselves, and our God. I appreciate the encouragement of Paul in his letters to the Ephesians where he instructs, *"Put on the full armor of God, so that when the day of evil comes, you may be able to stand your ground, and after you have done everything, to stand"* (Ephesians 6:13). When hopelessness and despair come in like a flood and you have done all you know to do, stand.

There is a gospel story that helps me when I don't know what to do. Jesus had just received the news that his cousin had been murdered. He was trying to get away from the crowd to spend some time alone with God in prayer, but the crowd followed. In his compassion, he taught and fed them before sending them and his disciples away. Later that night, in the middle of a terrible storm, he walked across the Sea of Galilee to where his disciples were struggling to stay afloat in their boat, and stilled the storm.

The next day, the multitudes found him again. Jesus knew they rejected his claim of being the Messiah and, instead, just wanted miracles and maybe a meal. So he pressed them and spoke of eternal life, and that to receive it, they must eat his flesh and drink his blood. He wasn't speaking of cannibalism, but it sure sounded like it to many.

Scripture says that *"from this time many of his disciples turned back and no longer followed him"* (John 6:66). I love what happened next. Jesus turned to his friends—the Twelve—looked them in the eye, and asked, *"You do not want to leave too, do you?"* (John 6:67). Peter beautifully answered, *"Lord, to whom shall we go? You have the words of eternal life.*

We have come to believe and to know that you are the Holy One of God" (John 6:68).

When hopelessness comes, stand on what you know to be true. In the case of Job, Job lost almost everything precious to him in a single day: his children, all assets, his business, and his good health. Hope was ripped from his life, and he was assaulted by despair. Remarkably, he responded to this assault with praise and worship, as follows: *"Naked I came from my mother's womb, and naked I will depart. The Lord gave and the Lord has taken away; may the name of the Lord be praised.' In all this, Job did not sin by charging God with wrongdoing"* (Job 1:21-22). His wife was understandably shaken, and, in her disappointment and despair, she advised Job to curse God and die. Job's response was again remarkable: *"You are talking like a foolish woman. Shall we accept good from God, and not trouble?"* (Job 2:10). The ultimate declaration of Job is found in Job 13:15:

"Though he slay me, yet will I hope in him."

Hope despite hopelessness. Job seems superhuman and his response unnatural. But Job was human like you and me, and his story provides testimony that hope can live in spite of our circumstances. The deepest valley and the darkest night aren't too big for hope. We can pray along with the psalmist, *"Even though I walk through the darkest valley, I will fear no evil, for you are with me; your rod and your staff, they comfort me"* (Psalm 23:4). Job's hope was not based on wealth, the condition of his family, nor on his health. It came from a place beyond all circumstances—it came from his relationship with God.

Job's is not the only testimony of those who clung to God and found hope against all odds. Horatio Spafford was a successful young lawyer and businessman in Chicago in the late 1800s. He was a devout Christian and a dear friend of D. L. Moody, a famous theologian and evangelist of the day. Horatio was also a devoted father and husband. During 1871 his first son died of pneumonia. Later that year he lost the majority of his wealth during the Great Chicago Fire.

Two years later, after working to rebuild his wealth and business, he and his family were planning a trip to Europe for a time of rest, as well as to join D. L. Moody on his evangelistic trip to England. Horatio sent his wife and four daughters on ahead of him while he stayed back for a few days to attend to some unexpected business challenges. On their journey, the ship on which they were sailing, the SS *Ville du Havre,* was struck by the *Loch Earn,* a British vessel, and sank in less than twelve minutes. All four children died, but Anna was saved by a passing boat. When she arrived on land, she wired her husband the message "Saved alone. What shall I do." Horatio sailed from America to join his grieving wife, and the captain of the ship notified him when they passed over the place where his children were lost. Thinking of them as safe with the Lord, at that point Horatio penned the words of the great hymn "It Is Well with My Soul."

The faith and hope in God of both Horatio and Job seem impossible. Nevertheless, I am reminded of what Jesus said, that *"what is impossible with man is possible with God"* (Luke 18:27).

Wait in Hope

> "We know that the whole creation has been groaning as in the pains of childbirth right up to the present time. Not only so, but we ourselves, who have the firstfruits of the Spirit, groan inwardly as we wait eagerly for our adoption to sonship, the redemption of our bodies. For in this hope we were saved. But hope that is seen is no hope at all. Who hopes for what they already have? But if we hope for what we do not yet have, we wait for it patiently" (Romans 8:22-25).

We wait on God. We wait for our adoption as sons and daughters. We wait for the redemption of our bodies. We wait eagerly. We wait patiently. And we wait in hope. We wait because as Peter declared, "Where else will we go?" We wait because of the promise *"they who wait for the Lord shall renew their strength; they shall mount up with wings like eagles; they shall run and not be weary; they shall walk and not faint"* (Isaiah 40:31 ESV).

Waiting isn't a passive activity; it typically denotes a state of readiness and availability. It includes expectation and eagerness for what is to come. Someone who is lying in wait is watching, preparing, and anticipating coming events. Waiting can include serving, as someone who waits on and supplies the wants and needs of others. Waiting is active.

Good things come to those who wait. Waiting requires patience, and patience requires perspective. Patience is a virtue for all time, yet it goes against the grain of our time. We are an impatient people who live in a world demanding patience. Crops don't grow instantly. A farmer plants in one season and harvests in another. Building anything of substance requires patience; whether a business, a home, a church, or a family, we patiently build all of them step by step, brick by brick, page by page, moment by moment. This perspective required by patience comes as we remind ourselves of who made and owns the seasons and at whose voice and command they change from one to the next.

Waiting, patience, and perspective are on display throughout Scripture and featured prominently in the teachings of Jesus. In the parable of the ten virgins, Jesus stressed the idea of preparation while waiting. The only difference between the two sets of virgins were those prepared for the wait and those who weren't. Waiting was required for both; however, the unprepared ones missed out altogether!

So we watch for God, and we prepare for him. With eagerness and anticipation, we look forward to the future. And while we wait, we also serve him and attend to him. Jude wrote, *"Keep yourselves in God's love as you wait for the mercy of our Lord Jesus Christ to bring you to eternal life"* (Jude 1:21). The psalmist David declared, *"Wait for the Lord; be strong and take heart and wait for the Lord"* (Psalm 27:14). We look up. We hope not in our current circumstances but in him. We hope in his coming kingdom and in whatever goodness comes our way as we wait.

Build Hope

So how do we build hope and prepare ourselves for the disappointments and hopeless situations that will affront us on our journeys? Jesus talked about how we build. He said we can hear his words and put them into practice, or we can hear his words and ignore them. Those are our two choices. If we hear and put them into practice, we are like builders who build on a foundation of rock; when difficulties come, whether rain, floods, or winds, our house stands. Or if we hear and ignore, we're like foolish builders who build on sand; when difficulties come, whether rain, floods, or winds, our house collapses. The storms are the same, but the results vastly differ based on how we build.

When God was laying out his plans and purposes to the children of Israel in the desert of Sinai, he told them, *"This day I call the heavens and the earth as witnesses against you that I have set before you life and death, blessings and curses. Now choose life, so that you and your children may live"* (Deuteronomy 30:19). Choice is a gift! Life will bring its share of storms and many reasons to lose hope. It is there that our choices determine our destiny. On what will we build, and on what will we focus? If we choose God, his words, and his ways, we have unending hope. The writer of the book of Hebrews describes this hope as *"an anchor for the soul, firm and secure"* (Hebrews 6:19).

Imagination

Building hope requires imagination. To have hope, imagine what you don't have and look forward to it, even though it doesn't yet exist. We have all heard stories from successful people in all walks of life about the role imagination played in their successful journey. Baseball players talk about seeing themselves hit a home run before they hit it. Quarterbacks envision a touchdown pass before they throw it. Architects see a building before it's built. Surgeons envision a surgery before they pick up their scalpel. On and on it goes. In many cases the imagination becomes so vivid, the dreamer becomes convinced of its reality before its very birth. The dream becomes so precious, so desired, and so clear that it births the reality of what was only a picture.

Albert Einstein had some important things to say about imagination. He said, "Imagination is more important than knowledge." Furthermore, this quote is attributed to him: "Imagination is everything. It is the preview of life's coming attractions." The opposite is also true: if you have no imagination, you have nothing; no vision for the future. Carl Sagan said, "Imagination will often carry us to worlds that never were. But without it we go nowhere." To hold hope, we must see beyond our circumstances. To see clearly, we must focus. And to focus, we must direct our gaze toward the thing we want to see. We don't look indiscriminately; we gaze intently. Then and only then will we see the object of our desire and attain the very thing for which we hope and dream.

Imagination is seeing the unseen. The apostle Paul described it this way: *"Hope that is seen is no hope at all. Who hopes for what they already have? But if we hope for what we do not yet have, we wait for it patiently"* (Romans 8:24-25). We live in the tension between two worlds; the world of our present circumstances and the world that is to come. This is the tension between now and not yet. If we lose sight of the not yet, we lose hope. So instead, we envision the coming world. We look to see what our future will be.

Count Blessings

As we focus on the unseen, another tool that helps us is counting our blessings. This practice of gratitude lifts our eyes from heartbreaks and disappointments and helps us find sunlight amidst the darkness. People who are grateful are more joyful, and joyful people are graced with strength. All of us can practice gratitude.

Practicing gratitude is like anything else—the more you do it, the better you become at it. Try to find something to be grateful for every day. If you struggle with this, start small. Pause now and be grateful that you're alive at this moment and for your very next breath. You just practiced gratitude and are on your way to a life of joy!

Trust in Hope

What is arguably the most well-known passage of Scripture confirms what our hearts knew all along.

"And now these three remain: faith, hope and love. But the greatest of these is love" (1 Corinthians 13:13).

The pillars of life rest on these three. And there, right in the center, is hope. John Eldredge labeled these the three great treasures of the human heart. The New Living Translation of this verse states that they will last forever. Each of them is so valuable and so immensely important that we hold extremely high ideals for them. However, the challenge comes in living them. Ideals are great, but they must be converted into action. Living these in the rough-and-tumble world of our human condition is much more gritty, muddy, and messy than we ever imagined.

In love, our ideal of a growing romance looks more like a daily decision. In faith, our ideal of an intimate relationship with God feels many days like "a long obedience in the same direction" as Eugene Peterson declared. In hope, the excitement of anticipation can wane into the heartsickness of hope deferred. The dissonance caused by the clash of ideals with our human condition can lead to great frustration and pain; yet, these are the great treasures of the human heart that we must not abandon.

When the Israelites of the Exodus were learning to trust God, most of the times their faith was tested, they failed. No one could deny that God was with Moses as God performed sign after sign, miracle after miracle, and plague after plague until the Egyptians could no longer deny the Israelites' release from bondage. God also gave them a constant reminder of his presence, guiding them as a pillar of cloud by day and giving them light as a pillar of fire by night. Then God opened the Red Sea for the Israelites to cross but closed the way for the Egyptians.

Even though God manifested his presence and aided the Israelites in all these tangible ways, when they encountered difficulty, they would complain and turn their hearts from God. They did encounter many difficulties; lack of water, lack of food, and even attacking armies, but God was there. He never promised everything would be easy; however, he desired that they follow him in trust and count on him to see them through.

God is present in our world and in our lives. He may not be as evident as plagues, parting of seas, manna from heaven, or pillars of cloud and fire, but he is present nonetheless. Knowing this, why do we choose to complain and doubt rather than trust? Moses told the Israelites when they faced the Egyptian army on one side and the Red Sea on the other, *"Do not be afraid. Stand firm and you will see the deliverance the Lord will bring you today. The Egyptians you see today you will never see again. The Lord will fight for you; you need only to be still"* (Exodus 14:13-14).

"Be still, and know that I am God" (Psalm 46:10).

These encounters with the treasures of life in the mud and mire of our human condition aren't easy. Again, God didn't promise they would be easy. In fact, he promised the exact opposite.

"I have told you these things, so that in me you may have peace.
In this world you will have trouble. But take heart!
I have overcome the world," said Jesus (John 16:33).

Don't be discouraged by the collision of ideals with reality. This is where we live, this is where we learn, and this is where we encounter God. When he doesn't make sense, when the odds are stacked against us, and when we are up against a wall, he is testing our hearts and he is measuring our faith, hope, and love. Remember, the greatest of these is love. And love always hopes!

CHAPTER 5

Celebration Matters

A few years ago as October approached, I found myself thinking of the season ahead. My birthday is in October, and just over a month later comes my wedding anniversary, sneaking in right before Thanksgiving. Around the corner comes Christmas, followed by the beginning of a brand-new year. As I contemplated these coming days, I realized how much opportunity I had to celebrate!

Overall, I'm a person who is happy and content. I'm also practical and realistic, and sometimes those attributes take the lead. If I'm not careful, instead of fully celebrating the moment, I'm off to the next. As I was considering the months ahead and all the special events, an invitation stirred in my heart. I sensed God inviting me into a season where I would discipline myself to celebrate. I know that may seem ironic and silly. However, for me, it was an exciting invitation filled with joy.

You see, I have always been a disciplined person. I was the kid who went to all my classes, did all my homework, and studied for all my tests. When I decided to learn to play the guitar, I practiced for thirty minutes a day. For my health, I regularly discipline my body with exercise. For work, I have a planner where I keep lists to help me follow through with the most important tasks of the day.

For disciplined people like me, if we're not careful, life can become a to-do list where we work on goals every day, checking our list to gauge progress. Times of celebration may make the list, but we check them off like we do most other things and move on. The challenge with lists is that we never get to the end! As we check items off, we add more on. The satisfying feeling of accomplishment is diminished by the constant realization of more to do. This applies to every area of our lives, including our families, work, communities, and even our spiritual lives. Realizing that our work is never done can lead us to discouragement and despair.

As I was contemplating God's invitation, I sensed God smiling while inviting me to trust him in a new way and experience a facet of life I hadn't fully encountered. I envisioned a twinkle in his eye as he invited me to celebrate.

How do we discipline ourselves to celebrate? It starts with slowing down and enjoying each moment. It means stopping to smell the roses, putting away the lists, and fully giving ourselves to celebration.

Bucket-List Celebration

Years ago, I decided to make a bucket list; a list of things I want to do before I finish my journey on earth. It's been fun to periodically read it through to see what I've been able to accomplish and what I still want to do. It has also helped me make decisions through the years. For instance, when I was invited to go scuba diving in Panama a few years ago, it helped that "go scuba diving again" was on my list. Though the trip was inconvenient and expensive, it was one of 132 items and was therefore important. Taking my family to see U2 on my forty-seventh birthday was a no-brainer because "seeing U2 in concert" was on my list. Likewise, I go to see James Taylor at every opportunity because "see James Taylor in concert again" made the list.

Carrie and I were able to celebrate our twenty-fifth wedding anniversary with a trip to Rome and Israel. Her parents had invited a small group of friends and family to join them there in celebration of their fiftieth wedding anniversary. They had been to Israel four times and had a love for the land and its people. The trip didn't come at a great time in our financial life or in our family's life, yet we had longed to visit Israel for as long as we could remember and "visit Israel" was the first item on my bucket list.

I'm learning that celebration is a choice, one that isn't easy but very important. I want to learn to celebrate more often, more freely, and more fully. As C. S. Lewis wrote, "Joy is the serious business of Heaven," and I want my life to be characterized by joy. Learning to celebrate has increased my joy!

Joy isn't conditional; it isn't based upon circumstances. In fact, joy supersedes circumstances. Joy can't be taken or stolen from you; it's deeper than that.

I believe many people live with "the grass is always greener on the other side" mentality. They are waiting for the day when . . .

> they finally graduate
>
> they land the promotion they have been hoping for
>
> they meet Mr. or Mrs. Right
>
> they pay off their debts
>
> they recover from an illness
>
> they receive the recognition they desire
>
> things improve at home

You fill in the blanks. When these things happen, then they will finally be happy. This scripture verse rings true: *"Hope deferred makes the heart sick"* (Proverbs 13:12). If we are always deferring celebration, we aren't living in celebration.

Cost of Celebration

All good things come at a price, and so it is with celebration. Sacrifices and trade-offs occur with anything. I like to call these sacrifices opportunity costs. Choosing to celebrate will cost me, specifically in time and money. Because celebration seems luxurious for those of us with a pragmatic bent, we push it to the bottom of the list. This becomes a problem because items at the bottom of our list usually stay there, or we eventually remove them from the list entirely. Yes, celebrations are costly. My scuba trip to Panama was a few thousand dollars, dollars not readily available. As always, many other things competed for those dollars at the time, not to mention the ever-present need to save for the future.

In addition, my trip meant time away from a demanding schedule at work as well as from my family. Furthermore, since I hadn't been scuba diving in over twenty-five years, I thought it necessary to take a refresher course to remember how to calculate dive tables and become comfortable with the equipment again. It was costly in terms of both time and money.

Four tickets to see U2 weren't cheap. Moreover, we spent about five to six hours of that October day on the highway between Tulsa and Norman due to the amount of traffic converging on Memorial Stadium. Like my scuba trip, this celebration was costly in both time and money!

Cost versus Investment

Of course celebration is costly—isn't everything of worth? Understanding the priority of celebration will help us to be willing to pay the price. If life is just about getting to the end of our days with more cash in our pockets or a larger bank account, then we should spend less on celebrating and more on saving. Yet, I believe we can all agree with this famous 1940s newspaper ad:

> "In the end, it's not the years in your life that count.
> It's the life in your years."

Celebration brings life. It gives us an opportunity to express ourselves and the things that are important to us. We pause from our routines and enter moments of celebration. Celebration is a way of expressing what matters most; the moments versus the money.

Maybe the language of cost is troublesome for you. Instead of viewing the price tag of celebration as an expense, let's reframe it as an investment. It isn't money spent and gone forever, but money invested in your life, in your loved ones, and in your heart. The return on the investment won't be strictly material but will come in the form of memories and shared experiences that no one can take away from you, experiences that will enrich your family and your friendships. Maybe this touches on the heart of what Jesus said when he discussed treasure:

> *"Don't collect for yourselves treasures on earth, where moth*
> *and rust destroy and where thieves break in and steal.*
> *But collect for yourselves treasures in heaven, where*
> *neither moth nor rust destroys, and where thieves*
> *don't break in and steal. For where your treasure is,*
> *there your heart will be also"* (Matthew 6:19-21 HCSB).

Jesus' friend Mary had the heart of celebration. She and her siblings had become followers of Jesus and embraced him as the Messiah. In addition, they had become his dear friends. When her brother Lazarus became sick, she sent word to Jesus of his illness and its urgency. But Jesus delayed, and Lazarus died. Though her heart was broken, she received more than she ever thought possible when four days later Jesus raised Lazarus from the dead!

A few days later, Mary and her family threw a dinner party in Jesus' honor. At the party, Mary arose and poured some very expensive perfume (worth a year's wages) on Jesus' feet. Its fragrance filled the home. What a picture of celebration! In celebrating Jesus, Mary showed where her heart was and what she valued. She so appreciated all that he had done for her and her family that she wanted to publicly honor and worship him. She even did this while knowing that the political and religious climate around them was charged by those plotting to kill Jesus, people who discredited his miracles and his words. She took her stand in celebration.

Those of the more practical sort decried this lavish expenditure and public display, exclaiming that the opportunity cost of her celebration was too high, and the money could have been better spent. I love the response of Jesus to such criticism. He said, *"You always have the poor with you, but you do not always have Me"* (John 12:8 HCSB). In other words, you can always be practical.

Go ahead and be practical if you choose, yet don't miss the more important moments of celebration. Don't miss the life in your years. This act of celebration was so important that in Matthew's telling of this story, he recorded Jesus as saying, *"Wherever this gospel is proclaimed in the whole world, what this woman has done will also be told in memory of her"* (Matthew 26:13 HCSB). Mary made a tremendous investment in celebration, from which she is still reaping rewards.

Reasons to Celebrate

We always have reasons to celebrate. Let's not miss or overlook them because of what we choose to think about and where we place our gaze. We can focus on many things—some good, some bad, and some neither. The choice of where we focus changes everything. Roadblocks exist to anything worthwhile, and if we focus on them, we won't find the detour.

We all know those who see the glass of life as half empty. Though true, I encourage you with the parallel truth that the glass is also half full. The more we concentrate on the water, the less we see the empty space. The important thing is where we place our focus, whether on the water or the empty space. If we see the water, then we have reason to celebrate.

In our quest for perfection, we long for conditions to improve. We believe that only once we achieve perfection can we then be satisfied; never in a million years could we celebrate a glass half full, for that would be settling for less than the best! However, the problem is that we never achieve perfection and are therefore caught in an endless cycle of always striving and never celebrating. I'm not suggesting that we compromise or lower the bar. I desire to accomplish great things, and I am sure you do too. To do so, we must exert great effort and discipline to achieve the goals we're pursuing. Accomplishing great things takes determination and an indomitable spirit. I, along with Paul, want to run the race to win it.

"Not that I have already obtained all this, or have already arrived at my goal, but I press on to take hold of that for which Christ Jesus took hold of me. Brothers and sisters, I do not consider myself yet to have taken hold of it. But one thing I do: Forgetting what is behind and straining toward what is ahead, I press on toward the goal to win the prize for which God has called me heavenward in Christ Jesus" (Philippians 3:12-14).

I encourage you to strive for greatness but not perfection and to keep a heart of celebration along the way. Celebrate the small steps, the incremental gains, and the little victories. We never know how long we have on this planet and where our journey will take us. I want to be one who stops and smells the roses or, at least, notices their beauty as I pass. Life is filled with wonder and beauty, and gazing on them changes and moves us. Don't miss it—if we don't gaze at the sky and stars, we'll miss the wonder!

Practical Ways to Celebrate

So find ways and reasons to celebrate. As you look for them, they will become evident. The axiom holds true that you will find what you are looking for.

"Ask and it will be given to you; seek and you will find; knock and the door will be opened to you" (Matthew 7:7).

A few years ago, I purchased a new car. Afterward, I began to notice more and more of the same make and model everywhere I went. I'm sure they were there before, but now that I was looking for them, I began to notice them more frequently. So it is with celebration: if you're looking for ways and reasons to celebrate, you will find them!

Practice Gratitude

One way to celebrate is to practice gratitude. If your heart and mind are set on blessings rather than on difficulties, you'll receive opportunities to celebrate. With each blessing you acknowledge, you'll foster a heart of gratitude. Start small by writing down things for which you are grateful. Some people keep a gratitude journal where they count blessings for a certain number of days to help shift their thinking. You can be grateful verbally, but there is power in the exercise of writing things down; it yields more permanence and engages the mind, heart, and memory more fully.

I am grateful today because . . .

I have a beautiful wife who loves me

I have two great kids

I was raised in a home of love and affection

I live in America, a country I love and a land of opportunity and freedom

I have good friends

I have a nice home

I have meaningful employment

I have hope

My mind is sharp, and I can write, read, learn, and reflect

I have gifts and strengths to offer others

I have a great dog that brings joy to our family

I love music and the creativity and gifts of others

I love the ocean

I enjoy exploring the world around me

Once you and I start counting, we'll find no end to the blessings we have encountered in life. Of course, we've encountered difficulties too, some substantial; but again, the more we choose to set our mind on our blessings, the more we'll foster a heart of thankfulness and a spirit of celebration.

Observe and Commemorate

Another practical way to celebrate is to observe special days and occasions. Drink deeply of birthdays and anniversaries, weddings and holidays. Mark special occasions and let special occasions mark you. If you think no days are special, I'm confident celebration doesn't come easy for you; yet, go ahead and mark days and moments of meaning to you by circling them on your calendar and anticipating them before they happen. Once they arrive, be present and enter them fully. Once they pass, nurture their memory through photographs, journal entries, and mementos.

When Carrie and I were newlyweds, we had the opportunity to celebrate our second Christmas together with her family in England. Since both Carrie and I had been born in England, this was particularly special for us. We visited the communities where our parents lived when we were born, and we were happy to see our former homes. Just down the street from my home in the town of Aldeburgh, I stepped onto the rocky beach of the North Sea and picked up a smooth rock. That rock still sits on my desk. Now when I pick up that rock from my British homeland, I remember the rocky beach, the colorful boats, and the misty, humid air. And I remember the place from which I got my start.

Since I picked up that very first rock, I've collected rocks from all over the world, from Nantucket to Alaska. Each rock reminds me of my journey. My friends and family have even added to my collection: Kellie brought a stone back from Myanmar, and a friend carried a rock back from Machu Picchu in Peru. One of my favorites is the rock from my visit to the Valley of Elah, the valley where David slew Goliath. When I hold it, I remember our trip, but I also think of the giants I face, and I long for the courage and faith to fight them like David did.

Carrie and I like to collect Christmas ornaments from special places we visit. Decorating our Christmas tree every year brings back memories of Christmases past and our journeys as a family. We've also decorated our game room with national park posters showing where we have explored as a family.

Now in my fifties, I'm amazed at how fast the years have gone by. They are like a vapor or a dream that passes much faster than we think. Even if celebrating doesn't come naturally to you, drink in the moments and the days. Celebrate the special ones. Observe and commemorate them. It isn't that we want to stay in the past, but that we want to remember and commemorate and give thanks for the blessings of our lives and our journeys.

Celebrate Others

In addition to observing and commemorating our own lives, it's important to celebrate others. That's why we visit hospitals to celebrate births, and attend birthday parties and weddings, bringing gifts and raising our glasses. We go to funerals to honor memories and mourn those we've lost.

We also celebrate with special church services on Easter and Christmas. We attend parades on Memorial Day and fireworks on the Fourth of July. And at the end of every year, as the page turns on the calendar, we keep vigil by watching the moments count down as the old year passes and the new year is birthed.

There are a million ways to remember and a million more ways to observe special occasions. I've only offered a handful of suggestions. Though you may not want to pick up rocks, I hope you have felt the power of commemorating and how it aids in fostering a heart of celebration.

"Teach us to number our days, that we may
gain a heart of wisdom" (Psalm 90:12).

The Art of Celebration

If celebration and joy are not your regular companions, I encourage you to make room for them. You've heard it said that success is a journey, not a destination. This holds true for celebration and joy. They are not a place to arrive, but a way of living that bring deeper meaning and fulfillment.

By choosing to celebrate and by recognizing its importance, you will find more and more opportunities to do so, both in your life and in the lives of others. Celebration will become your way of life, and the fruit of joy will manifest and provide strength for you and those around you as well.

CHAPTER 6

Work Matters

*The earth and everything in it, the world and its inhabitants,
belong to the Lord.*

—Psalm 24:1 CSB

As the old hymn declares, this is my Father's world. Everything seen and unseen was birthed from his heart and belongs to him. The deep waters of the Pacific, the thundering herds of the Great Plains, the tall mountain passes of the Rockies, the bedrock of Mount Zion, the dark of the deepest jungle, the waves of the North Atlantic, and the far reaches of the Milky Way—these all belong to him. They are his creation and design. The soaring eagle, the beautiful cardinal, the playful otter, the darting hummingbird, the lion, the tiger, the mountains, and the valleys are all his. And the list is incomplete without you and me.

Why do we live as if we have no purpose? And why do we live as if we belong to ourselves? Both are misplaced ideas. Scripture states, *"In the beginning you laid the foundations of the earth, and the heavens are the work of your hands"* (Psalm 102:25). Another passage declares, *"You, Lord, are our Father. We are the clay, you are the potter; we are all the work of your hand"* (Isaiah 64:8). God is not a faulty designer, and he doesn't make mistakes. He also doesn't do anything by chance or accident. Since everything belongs to him, how should we live, and what should be our response?

Gratefulness

We are all recipients of the gift of life, and, as with all gifts, our first response should be thanks. To have a heart of thankfulness and gratefulness for whatever blessings we have received is good and right. I've counseled my kids to refrain from boasting or taking pride in whatever gifts they have, whether regarding their appearance, intelligence, or any other gift. As the apostle Paul says in his letter to the Corinthian church, *"What do you have that you did not receive? And if you received it, why do you boast as if it were not a gift?"* (1 Corinthians 4:7 NRSV). One temptation with gifts is to hold on to them too tightly. This is the danger of materialism. Since all belongs to God and is safely in his hands, we should be grateful and loosely hold our gifts.

Stewardship and Enjoyment

Since God has plans and purposes for everything, I believe stewardship is our second appropriate response. We are stewards of God's world, but more than that, we are his family, and he crafted the world not just for our stewardship but also our enjoyment.

When God placed Adam in the garden, he gave him authority over everything and encouraged him to work and to take care of it. This call to stewardship was not a curse but a call to enter the work and be a cocreator with God. As God's family, the world is our inheritance. One of the best things about gifts is that they are given to be enjoyed. When I give gifts to my family, I give something I hope they will really like or have been wanting. I want to bless them, and so it is with God's gifts to us.

God has things for us to do, places for us to discover, and people for us to be connected to. I believe this is the abundant life Jesus was talking about when he said, *"I have come that they may have life, and have it to the full"* (John 10:10). Jesus described the goodness of the Father and his intentions toward us when he was discussing prayer with his disciples.

'Ask and it will be given to you; seek and you will find; knock and the door will be opened to you. For everyone who asks receives; the one who seeks finds; and to the one who knocks, the door will be opened. "Which of you, if your son asks for bread, will give him a stone? Or if he asks for a fish, will give him a snake? If you, then, though you are evil, know how to give good gifts to your children, how much more will your Father in heaven give good gifts to those who ask him! So in everything, do to others what you would have them do to you, for this sums up the Law and the Prophets.' (Matthew 7:7-12)

As we receive all the good gifts our heavenly Father has for us, we need to keep in mind that we don't have to cling to any of these things nor push and pull for our own way. Instead, we look to him and ask for understanding of the small role we play in this grand world he created for our pleasure and enjoyment. Gary Barkalow says it well in his book on our personal calling entitled *It's Your Call* when he writes, "The discovery of what God has created us to do is a matter of asking, seeking, and knocking. The discoverable clues about who we are can be found only as we resist the shallows and prefer the deep. We are to be explorers and archaeologists, not tourists and visitors."

It's important to remember that this is our Father's world. As Francis Schaeffer said in *The God Who Is There*, "Regardless of a man's system, he has to live in God's world." Two scripture verses reminding me of our need to stay connected with God and his purposes and not our own are Psalm 127:1-2: *"Unless the Lord builds the house, the builders labor in vain. Unless the Lord watches over the city, the guards stand watch in vain. In vain you rise early and stay up late, toiling for food to eat—for he grants sleep to those he loves."*

Stewardship carries with it the idea of faithfulness and trust. Paul wrote in 1 Corinthians 4:2, *"It is required of stewards that they be found trustworthy"* (RSV). Our proper response as stewards and children of God should be faithfulness. May we faithfully steward our lives and be found trustworthy for all that is placed in our care. First and foremost, this includes the precious gift of life, but it extends from there to everything else, including our planet, the nations, our families, communities, resources, and jobs.

Fruitfulness and Productivity

All good fathers want the best for their kids and want them to excel in every way. A good dad wants his ceiling to be his children's floor, and for them to live fruitful and fulfilling lives. When I think of my own kids, my desire for them is not that they choose a specific profession. My hope is that they live lives of meaning and purpose and that they find happiness. I hope that they walk with love in their hearts toward their fellow man, that they live with character and conviction, and that they encounter the love of God so they can offer it to others. I hope they have successful marriages. I hope they have children on whom to lavish their love, and I hope they find meaningful work that makes a contribution to others and that can provide a means for them to build a financial future.

Our heavenly Father longs for all of us to be fruitful. He longs for us to see better days. He longs for us to have meaningful work that stirs our heart and imagination. He longs for us to grow financially and to be able to provide for our families, communities, and others in need. He longs for us to succeed. He is crazy about us and wants us to be happy.

God's admonition to be fruitful found in Genesis 1 is not an isolated command. Jesus also talked about it in his famous teaching on the vine and the branches found in John 15. In this passage, he says that he is the vine, the Father is the gardener, and we as children are the branches of the vine. The gardener tends the vine, looking for fruit. Branches that are connected to the vine will be fruitful, and branches that aren't connected will die. He ends the passage by saying that it is to his Father's glory that branches bear much fruit (see v. 8).

This passage is helpful for me in many ways. John 15:5 reminds me that apart from him, I can do nothing, and that I must remain in him to be fruitful. This shouldn't come as a surprise, as even Jesus said that he could do nothing apart from his Father (see John 5:19). If my fruit is dependent upon my remaining in him, my focus can become simple: Jesus. In pursuing a relationship with God through the person of his Son, I am pursuing the abundant life my heart longs for. If I remain in him and keep my heart and eyes fixed on him, I'm less likely to get distracted and satisfied with materialism and self-seeking with all their trinkets and toys.

Additionally, it is helpful to remember that my fruit is God's decision. Apple trees produce apples, and lemon trees, lemons. An apple tree cannot produce whatever fruit it wants, and so it is with us. We were designed and created by God for fruitfulness with the fruit he designed. Offer whatever fruit you produce, whether wisdom, encouragement, or joy to those around you. Don't be discouraged that you produce only "apples." Instead, rejoice in the apples that fall from your branch.

Jesus again stressed the importance of fruitfulness near the end of his ministry. The timing of his delivery emphasized its importance. As he approached Jerusalem on his last trip before his betrayal, Jesus saw a fig tree and started walking over to it, hoping to eat its fruit. When he got close, he realized it had no figs, and he cursed it. This is an odd story, but it puts an exclamation point on the fact that God desires fruit. Because he made a fig tree for figs, if it has no fruit, its purpose has died. Life had already left the tree, though the tree was not technically dead. We have all seen many individuals in the same condition; though not dead, they are without purpose or fruitfulness.

I love the passage in Ephesians 2 that states, *"For we are God's handiwork, created in Christ Jesus to do good works, which God prepared in advance for us to do"* (v. 10). I love that it speaks of such intentionality, confirming that our heavenly Father prepared specific works for us. He has things for us to do, and fruit for us to produce. I also love this prayer of the psalmist: *"May the favor of the Lord our God rest on us; establish the work of our hands for us—yes, establish the work of our hands"* (Psalm 90:17).

Work That Matters

Jesus brought his Father glory by finishing the work he was given to do (see John 17:4). We can do the same. My pastor recently described the scene in Luke 10 where Jesus sent out thirty-six teams of followers to prepare cities for his visit. He coached them, then sent them off to work. They returned with amazing reports of healings and deliverances. My pastor described Jesus' response as similar to his when his son hit a grand slam at a recent baseball game; Jesus erupted with clapping, shouting, and celebrating, or as some would say, hooting and hollering.

Like all good fathers, God is cheering for his kids and is proud of our achievements. Like anything in life, there are always levels of achievement; good, better, and best. Though our Father is proud of all accomplishments, I believe he celebrates lavishly when we hit the home runs.

Let us live boldly and venture to enter his perfect will for our lives. Let us dare to be among those rare souls who reach for our inheritance, desiring what he has for us. Let us dare to believe, as Paul wrote, that eye has not seen, nor ear heard, nor has it entered into the human mind what God has prepared for those who love him (see 1 Corinthians 2:9). I don't believe this is limited to heaven. I believe it also means entering fully into the life and purposes he created for us on earth.

We have work to do, and our work matters. Our Father is fully invested in our success and celebrates our accomplishments. This is the "well done" response in the parable of the talents.

> *"His master replied, 'Well done, good and faithful servant! You have been faithful with a few things; I will put you in charge of many things. Come and share your master's happiness!'"* (Matthew 25:21).

I love the phrase "work that matters." I want to be doing that kind of work. I want it to matter to God, to me, and to those who come into contact with it. It may not be deserving of a standing ovation, but how awesome would it be if it was!

My favorite singer is James Taylor, and I have had the privilege of seeing him in concert on many occasions. The truth is, if he comes to Tulsa or the surrounding area, I will be there. He works with such grace and ease and I absolutely love his music. I have rewarded him with a standing ovation every time I've seen him.

I want to live in such a way that people want more of what I have to offer. If I were a performer, the reward of a job well done might be a standing ovation. In my line of work, I hope that people trust me and choose to do business with me and the organizations with which I am affiliated. I hope that I provide value and that they will choose the goods and services I provide over those of others. Ultimately, I desire that they will delight in doing business with me and that their lives are enriched because of it.

In June 2013, I had the privilege of seeing Paul McCartney in concert. The legendary Beatle was nearing his seventy-first birthday, and I was amazed as he sang for three hours without a break. He and his band performed thirty-eight songs, including two encores, in an unbelievable performance. I was so inspired by it that, in the weeks following, I purchased some of his live recordings so I could relive the evening.

I have enjoyed Paul's music since I was a kid, and he was my favorite Beatle. Knowing he has performed music in a career spanning more than fifty years, what captured my imagination that evening was his love and passion for his work. He surely doesn't need the money. So why in the world in his seventies is he continuing to travel the world singing his songs? I believe the answer is that he is doing what he was created to do. Watching him perform for three hours, his passion, joy, and fulfillment were evident. Likewise, when we do the work that we were made to do, I believe we will find passion, joy, and fulfillment.

Our work is not solely about money. Neither are most of the important things in life, including health, family, faith, friendship, and love. These things all supersede money. I am not intending to downplay the significance of money and its importance in providing for your life and family. However, I believe work that matters supersedes money. I have realized that what constitutes hitting home runs for me, which is another way of saying work that matters, is typically something that involves positively influencing others in relationships.

Finding Our Place

A single piece of a jigsaw puzzle provides a vivid picture of how each life matters in a unique way. First, no two pieces in the box are cut alike, each one unique in shape and image. Each piece is also made to be connected to other unique pieces, and to not stand alone. Still the pieces cannot be placed randomly. Instead, each piece fits perfectly with three or four others which the puzzle maker intentionally crafted. If I examine one piece by itself, I'm clueless about what picture it carries. However, as I connect piece to piece, the picture becomes clearer. Once complete, the picture is crystal clear.

We were made for community and not for isolation. At the same time, we cannot be all things to all people. Just like the puzzle piece, I believe God has particular people and places for us. If we're out of place, there is a hole in the puzzle that will never be filled until we find our spot.

Abundance versus Scarcity

As we find our place, we improve not only our lives but we, in turn, improve the lives of everyone around us. As those adjoining us find their places, more clarity comes. Finding my place assists others in finding theirs, each piece providing help to the next. As the saying goes, "A rising tide lifts all boats." I find that it truly does.

This idea is one of abundance rather than scarcity. The abundance mentality believes that there is enough for all and a place for all and that no one should be left out. The scarcity mentality believes the opposite; that we find our place in competition with each other. It believes that my success means your failure due to limited available resources. This is not the case. We all need each other to find our place, and the picture will be incomplete until we do. God's story will not be properly told if you don't find your way.

The Way Opens Up

As you consider your piece and your place, a helpful question to ask yourself is, "What do I want?" At certain times and in specific circumstances, the answer comes easily. If you're a student, the answer may be to pass today's test. If you're a businessman, today's answer may be to close the deal. If you're a parent dealing with a sick child, the answer may be healing and recovery for your child. The question is easier in the present moment when facing a test, a deal, or an illness. The real challenge comes in moments of reflection when taking a bigger inventory of life.

Others may assist, but, ultimately, we must each voice our own answer. In my experience, the answer doesn't come easily, as it requires mining the depths of my heart. I've heard it said that it takes God to know God. I believe this is true about our hearts as well. We must take the issues of our hearts and set them before God. We must ask for his guidance and his help to discern our way. I believe that as we do, as the Quaker saying goes, "The way will open."

Do the Next Right Thing

As you pursue your work and your place, and as you wrestle with the question of what it is you want, walk in the understanding that you have, do your best, and do the next right thing. Take the next step you know to take. With each step, just as happens to a miner with a light on his helmet, the way will light up before you. You won't see the full journey, but you'll see enough to continue.

Two of my favorite scripture verses from the earliest years of my faith journey are Proverbs 3:5-6, which say, *"Trust in the Lord with all your heart, and lean not on your own understanding; In all your ways acknowledge Him, and He shall direct your path"* (NKJV). These verses have brought me great comfort through the years. They have encouraged me to trust God and to rely on him rather than on myself. Finally, they acknowledge what I have always longed to be true; that if I do these things, then he will direct my steps, and I will find the life he has for me. He will put my puzzle piece in the right spot, at the right time, with the right people.

As I take each step, I am getting closer to God's perfect will for me. I may not understand everything, but I can trust that God is leading the way. If you're still confused over what is the next right thing to do, do the last thing you knew you should do. This may have come as an answer to prayer or as a result of a soul-searching exercise. Or maybe you don't know where it came from, but for some reason it is on your heart to do. Do it until you have clarity to do something else.

How to Work

So work matters, and what we do matters. But how we do what we do matters more! How we work speaks to our character. The end does not justify the means. If the result of our work were the only important thing, we could justify all kinds of bad behavior. These could include lying, stealing, and cheating; all sins and flaws that diminish and deplete, rather than help us to be fruitful, productive, and successful individuals. How we work is vital to our success.

You can read a library of books on the topic of character. For my purpose, I want to share just a few simple ideas on how we should work. I believe we should work hard, I believe we should work enthusiastically, and I believe we should work wholeheartedly.

Work Hard

There is much value in hard work, in the rolling up of your sleeves and diving into whatever is in front of you. Nothing satisfies like a job well done. The completion of a task in which you are invested is reward in and of itself.

Work Enthusiastically

Enthusiasm is contagious. Even if the work is tedious and generates little enthusiasm on its own merit, someone with enthusiasm can revolutionize it. I have seen people with talent and little enthusiasm, and I have seen people with little talent and great enthusiasm. We need to use our talent, without question, but if I had to choose between the two, I would take the enthusiastic individual.

Work Wholeheartedly

Since our heart is the most important thing about us, we should fully live from our hearts in our work life. It's easy to segment our lives and reserve our heart for the things that matter most to us. For many people, work is just a job, like a necessary evil endured for the result—the paycheck. Scripture speaks to this. In his letter to the Colossian church, Paul writes,

"Don't work only while being watched, in order to please men, but work wholeheartedly, fearing the Lord. Whatever you do, do it enthusiastically, as something done for the Lord and not for men, knowing that you will receive the reward of an inheritance from the Lord. You serve the Lord Christ" (Colossians 3:22-24 HCSB).

Likewise, Ecclesiastes 9:10 states, *"Whatever your hand finds to do, do it with all your might."* Work changes when you're all in and fully invested. So give it your all. Work as unto God. Work hard. Work enthusiastically. Work wholeheartedly.

Never Give Up

Finally, never give up and never quit! No matter how dire your circumstances or how faint the light at the end of the tunnel, never stop doing all you know to do. I don't want my life to fade away, I want it to end in a crescendo. I want to move closer to fulfilling my dreams and improve at stewarding all the Father has given me. How about you? It's never over until you quit. As long as you have breath in your lungs and the power to act and choose, keep fighting, keep loving, keep working, keep praying, keep exploring, and keep on keeping on.

One of my favorite movies is *Rudy*. I'm sure you know the story of the young man who, from childhood, loved Notre Dame football and dreamed of playing there one day. Against all odds and against many setbacks and disappointments, he made it to the campus of Notre Dame. He never officially made the football team but did become a practice squad player. Before the final home game of his senior year, the other players lobbied for him to dress with the team, and the coach agreed. As fate would have it, Notre Dame won the game by such a wide margin that the coach decided to let every senior play, including Rudy. Rudy made it onto the field as a Notre Dame football player.

This accomplishment may not seem like much to you and me, but for a young man who longed to play on that field with that team his entire life, it was a dream come true. All the disappointments and setbacks paled in comparison to the fulfillment of that dream. You might never accomplish all that is in your heart, but you can get close. Remember, if you don't aim for anything, you're guaranteed to miss.

"The credit belongs to the man who is actually in the arena,
whose face is marred by dust and sweat and blood;
who strives valiantly; who errs, who comes short again
and again . . . who knows the great enthusiasms,
the great devotions; who spends himself in a worthy cause;
who at the best knows in the end the triumph of
high achievement, and who at the worst, if he fails,
at least fails while daring greatly"
(Teddy Roosevelt).

CHAPTER 7

Vision Matters

Back in spring 2013, I was preparing for a spiritual retreat. My son, Luke, was about to graduate from high school, and I asked if he wanted to tag along for the weekend. I was so pleased when he said yes! We drove to my favorite retreat spot in Northwest Arkansas and settled in for a few nights. The purpose of the getaway was to set aside space to meet with God. For me, such times typically include time in Scripture, time in prayer, time journaling, and many walks in the woods. This weekend was particularly special having Luke with me. We didn't talk much, but I made myself available and let him know if he wanted to talk, I was there.

We each spent time alone in the woods with our journals, Bibles, and thoughts. Nearing the end of our time, I was praying about vision for the future. A famous proverb on vision that many Christians quote from memory is this: *"Where there is no vision, the people perish"* (Proverbs 29:18 KJV). I was pondering this and asking the Father for more vision for my life. This hasn't happened to me often, but, in that moment, I instantly believed God answered my prayer: my thoughts went to the old hymn "Be Thou My Vision."

> Be thou my vision, O Lord of my heart;
> naught be all else to me, save that thou art—
> thou my best thought, by day or by night;
> waking or sleeping, thy presence my light.

Be thou my wisdom, and thou my true word;
I ever with thee and thou with me, Lord;
thou my great Father, I thy true son;
thou in me dwelling, and I with thee one.
Riches I heed not, nor man's empty praise;
thou mine inheritance, now and always:
thou and thou only, first in my heart,
High King of heaven, my treasure thou art.
High King of heaven, my victory won,
may I reach heaven's joys, O bright heaven's Sun!
Heart of my own heart, whatever befall,
still be my vision, O Ruler of all.

(Trinity Psalter Hymnal #446, translated by Mary E. Byrne)

The words immediately resonated in my heart, and I knew this hymn was a gift from God and an answer to my prayer. So many phrases of this song touched how I wanted to live my life. In these lyrics, God had provided all the vision I needed.

As I contemplated the song, I became curious about its origin. I discovered that it was written as a poem in the sixth century and attributed to Saint Dallán Forgaill (AD 530-598), nicknamed "little blind one." How interesting that prayer for vision for my future was answered by a blind saint from the ancient past!

Do you have vision for your life? I believe you understand that I'm not talking about physical sight. I am talking about an ability to see what is beyond your natural vision. I am describing a vision to see with your mind's eye and your heart what is beyond current existence, to see what is to come and what may be. Yet, I'm not talking about just using your imagination, for imagination can deal in fantasy. I'm talking about vision to see things beyond surface appearances, to see things as they really are.

Physical sight can be a hindrance to the vision I'm describing. Many times what is directly in front of us distracts us from what is around us. Likewise, many times we focus on the minutiae and miss the bigger vista; we miss the forest for the trees. I'm reminded of the story where God revealed the plans of one of Israel's enemies, the king of Aram, to the prophet Elisha. Due to this revelation, Elisha was able to convey the secret plans to the king of Israel, who then saved his troops. When the king of Aram realized Elisha was spoiling his plans, he set out to attack Elisha. Elisha and his servants awoke to find themselves surrounded by a formidable fighting force of soldiers, horses, and chariots. One servant cried out to Elisha, "What are we going to do? Elisha replied, *"Don't worry about it— there are more on our side than on their side"* (2 Kings 6:16 MSG).

Then Scripture says that Elisha prayed for God to open the servant's eyes and let him see. And do you know what he saw? *"A wonder! The whole mountainside full of horses and chariots of fire surrounding Elisha!"* (2 Kings 6:17 MSG). Elisha's servant was previously distracted by what was directly in front of him: the Aramean army. His focus was on the enemy forces. Elisha prayed for vision for his friend so that he would see what was really going on—the true picture, the bigger vision. Things were not as they appeared to the servant's physical eyesight.

Seeing Differently

I want to see differently. Have you ever noticed that some people can see things others miss? Billy Crockett is attributed with saying this about his friend Rich Mullins: "What I loved best about Rich were his eyes. He could see things. Any decent painter would say it isn't about brush and texture, it's about seeing. Here is a man who wrote an epic praise song on the color green." I have good eyesight and am a rather curious individual. Even so, I bet that I'm missing many things as I walk around each day; things hidden, like songs in the color green, and other things staring me right in the face.

I read a story about Jesus recently that has stirred my imagination and my desire to see differently. The story takes place shortly after Jesus heard the news that his cousin John was beheaded. Jesus withdrew, seeking a solitary place to pray. But he was followed by a crowd of over five thousand people, and Scripture says, *"He had compassion on them and healed their sick"* (Matthew 14:14). As the day progressed and turned into night, the disciples encouraged Jesus to dismiss the crowd so they could go to surrounding villages and find something to eat. Jesus said to his disciples, *"They do not need to go away. You give them something to eat"* (v. 16). The disciples explained to him that they had only five loaves of bread and two fish, insufficient supplies at best. Jesus then said, *"Bring them here to me"* (v. 18). Jesus saw a feast among these sparse supplies. He saw a song in the color green.

I want to see like that. I'm encouraged that Jesus invited his friends into this mystery: *"They do not need to go away. You give them something to eat."* And I'm encouraged that Jesus performed the miracle with what was in their hands. He didn't create food out of nothing. He multiplied what they had.

What is in your hands? When you're facing an impossible situation, can you bring what is in your hands to Jesus, trusting that it's enough? For Moses, it was a shepherd's staff. With that humble staff, God performed great and mighty wonders and miracles throughout the land of Egypt and when the Israelites wandered through the desert of Sinai. For the widow of Zarephath in the middle of a famine and drought, it was only a handful of flour in a jar and a bit of olive oil in a jug. She offered those to Elijah the prophet of God, and her supply of oil and flour never ran out. For David, it was stones and a slingshot, his tools as a shepherd. He offered those to God when he faced Goliath, the giant armored warrior, and won for Israel its mightiest battle against its fiercest enemy. All these miracles, like the feeding of the five thousand, began by offering to God the very thing that was in one's hands, however humble or ill-equipped it seemed.

Don't despise or dismiss the thing in your hands, regardless of how inconsequential or insignificant. Instead, bring it to Jesus with a trusting heart, expecting the miracle he is waiting to do through your humble offering.

Don't Fear

> We're born with everything we'll ever need.
>
> —Jack Dorsey

You are enough and have all that you need. Many of us struggle believing this. Please know that everyone fights feelings of inadequacy and insufficiency. This applies as equally to vision as to everything else in life. Yet I encourage you to take comfort in the most common admonition found in Scripture: Don't fear. I encourage you to lean into God, to know that he is near and that he is for you. I encourage you to place your hope in God, to seek him and to trust that he has vision for you. Trust that his vision for your life will not fail but rather prevail. Believe in him. Believe in yourself.

> *"So is my word that goes out from my mouth: It will not return to me empty, but will accomplish what I desire and achieve the purpose for which I sent it"* (Isaiah 55:11).

> *"Not a single one of all the good promises the Lord had given to the family of Israel was left unfulfilled; everything he had spoken came true"* (Joshua 21:45 NLT).

Seek Vision

Vision starts with God. I encourage you to seek vision by seeking the God who imparts vision. The simple act of prayer is where it begins. It is where it began for me that day in 2013 on the retreat with Luke. A simple prayer. A simple request to God. A request for vision. And the answer comes. It doesn't always come immediately like it did that day. Those days are truly amazing. However, the answer does come. God longs to answer your prayer, particularly concerning vision. He has plans and purposes specifically designed for you. He longs to develop a relationship with you and reveal himself to you as you pursue him. There are many scripture verses supporting this idea. Let me share with you just a few of my favorites.

> *"Call to me and I will answer you and tell you great and unsearchable things you do not know"* (Jeremiah 33:3).

> *"For I know the plans I have for you,"* declares the Lord,
> *"plans to prosper you and not to harm you,*
> *plans to give you hope and a future"* (Jeremiah 29:11).

> *"For it is God who works in you to will and to act in order to fulfill his good purpose"* (Philippians 2:13).

> *"For we are God's handiwork, created in Christ Jesus to do good works, which God prepared in advance for us to do"* (Ephesians 2:10).

As you seek vision, seek first the God of vision and he will impart it to you. Keep in mind that he started this whole thing anyway. He created all of life, and only in him do we live and move and have our being (see Acts 17:28). Our breath is from him, and our days are a gift from him. And before you were born, he ordained your days and laid out plans and visions for your life (see Psalm 139:13-16; Jeremiah 1:5). So ask him in faith, and look to him for the vision for your life.

"I will instruct you and teach you in the way you should go; I will counsel you with my loving eye on you. Do not be like the horse or the mule, which have no understanding but must be controlled by bit and bridle or they will not come to you" (Psalm 32:8-9).

"But the plans of the Lord stand firm forever, the purposes of his heart through all generations" (Psalm 33:11).

It Will Be Done

I'm not sure how God's plan for you will be accomplished or when it will be accomplished or in what manner it will be accomplished, but it will be accomplished. You are God's son or daughter. If you are asking God for his leading and guidance, you can be assured he is there, leading and guiding, like he promised. You may not understand all the places he leads nor all that you encounter. However, as early-church father Saint John Chrysostom is attributed with saying, "A comprehended God is no God."

As you trust God with your vision, place all your confidence in him, not in your understanding of your vision or how it will be accomplished. If your life is anything like mine, I assure you it will look different than you imagine. Yet, *"I remain confident of this: I will see the goodness of the Lord in the land of the living. Wait for the Lord; be strong and take heart and wait for the Lord"* (Psalm 27:13-14).

Vision Is God's Delivery System

When we review the sacred pages of Scripture, we realize that vision is God's delivery system. From one end of the book to the other, God used visions to deliver his messages to anyone who had ears to hear. Examples include the visions of Daniel, Ezekiel, and Isaiah. Zechariah had a vision of an angel in the temple announcing his son. Peter, James, and John had a vision of Moses and Elijah on the Mount of Transfiguration. John the Baptist saw the Holy Spirit descend upon Jesus at the Jordan River. Cornelius had a vision in prayer and, in response, so did Peter. Mary Magdalene saw angels at the tomb of Jesus. On the road to Damascus, Paul had a vision of Jesus, and, on the island of Patmos, John the Beloved had a vision of Jesus and of heaven. On all these occasions, God was speaking to his people and revealing himself to them. When God has a word for you, he knows how to find you and is faithful to deliver it. And many times he delivers it through visions.

Vision Is Revealed

Vision is not something we generate for ourselves. Many people talk of writing vision statements for their lives. Those may be great exercises and helpful on many fronts. However, the greater vision for our lives is something shown to us by our heavenly Father. He gives it to us as a gift. Every good thing I have has come to me as a blessing from God, as a gift. I don't internally generate it, just like I didn't create my own sight. It was a gift. So it is with vision.

Late in his life, one of Jesus' closest friends was living in exile on a deserted island when he received a vision from God. This was a gift given to him externally. Vision for our lives, while not as dramatic, also comes to us from God, if we have the eyes to see it. Unlike natural gifts that we use without thinking—gifts such as sight, hearing, taste, smell, and touch— the vision that I am speaking of is a gift that we must receive, open, and believe before we can enjoy its benefits.

Many Miss Vision

Many miss the messages that come through vision. The crowd at a festival in Jerusalem the day Jesus said, *"Father, glorify your name!"* thought they heard thunder instead of hearing the voice from heaven that responded, *"I have glorified it, and will glorify it again"* (John 12:28). On the road to

Damascus, Paul was blinded by the light of Jesus and conversed with him, while his traveling companions heard only noise but didn't see anyone.

Jesus Invites Us to See

I take great comfort that Jesus invites us into vision. He invites us to ask, to seek, and to knock. He tells us to keep our eyes open and to look, to stand at the crossroads and ask for his ways (see Jeremiah 6:16). He encourages us by saying that he has placed before us open doors to which he alone holds the keys. Doors for us that no one can shut. He then stands at our doors and knocks and knocks. He wants us to open the doors to find him, to find his vision. He knows our weaknesses and our frailties. And he offers his Holy Spirit to aid us in our weaknesses and shortcomings. When we don't know what to pray, he prays for us. When we can't see, Jesus encourages us to purchase from him salve for our eyes to assist with our blindness (see Revelation 3:18). And the cost is free (see Isaiah 55:1).

God's Vision Will Not Fail

God's vision will come to pass and not one word will fail. You may not know when, where, or how, but it will come. I encourage you to look for it, to pray for it, and to embrace it when you find it. Life is an unfolding. As you pursue vision, you will receive bits and pieces in your quest. There will be times of great clarity, as I had that day on the prayer path, and other moments of mere glimpses, where vision seems more like shadows. Life is a knowing in part and an understanding in part. Move in what you know. Run with the vision that you have. More will come.

"You know with all your heart and soul that not one of all
the good promises the Lord your God gave you has failed.
Every promise has been fulfilled; not one has failed"
(Joshua 23:14).

"The Lord said to me, 'You have seen correctly, for I am watching to see that my word is fulfilled'" (Jeremiah 1:12).

I encourage you to grow in confidence that our heavenly Father is accomplishing his purposes on the earth and in your life. You may feel insignificant and wonder why God would include you in his vision or why he would have vision for you. I understand, as I have felt like that many times myself. But that is how good God is. That is how much he loves you. As you catch a glimpse of vision, offer the same humble prayer that Mary prayed when she said, *"May your word to me be fulfilled"* (Luke 1:38). Then watch and wait for his vision to be fulfilled. Run with what you know, and wait for God to clarify the rest. In due season, when the time is right, he will.

"Being confident of this, that he who began a good work in you will carry it on to completion until the day of Christ Jesus" (Philippians 1:6).

Have patience with yourself and with God. Place your trust in him and in his vision, even when it seems at odds with the world around you. Why? Because God has done it in the past, and God will do it again. God never changes.

"I the Lord do not change" (Malachi 3:6).

"Every good and perfect gift is from above, coming down from the Father of the heavenly lights, who does not change like shifting shadows" (James 1:17).

Write It Down

The best way to remember something is to write it down. I have found it true that out of sight is out of mind. Even though we have many electronic aids in our day, I still use a paper day planner. The day planner keeps a written list before me of things I have chosen as important for today, tomorrow, and the future. It helps me to focus on what I am working on and what I want to accomplish. It also helps me keep track of the important dates ahead of me.

I also like to journal. It is not so much that I enjoy the practice of writing things down, as this takes time and discipline, but I do it so I don't forget. I don't want to forget people; I don't want to forget their names or why and how I met them. I don't want to forget meaningful places I've been to and the experiences I've had. Most importantly, I don't want to forget the thoughts that have stirred my heart.

In both my planner and my journal are notes on vision. The vision received from the Lord is scribbled throughout. Each day in my planner, I am attempting to take some action toward the fulfillment of the vision; the action may be small, but it is movement nonetheless. I can tell you with certainty that if I didn't write it down, I would quickly forget it, and other priorities would replace it. Life is filled with noise. If you're not keeping vision ever in front of you and taking steps to fulfill that vision, you are working to fulfill someone else's vision.

Vision won't be fulfilled without great intention and effort. Yes, the vision itself is a gift to you, but its fulfillment will not come without blood, sweat, and tears. As with all precious things, fulfilling the vision comes at a high price. That is why recording your vision in writing and keeping it ever before you is so important. Make weekly entries in your planner, write dates on your calendar, and place words related to your vision on your desk or in your art or on your computer screen saver. Place Post-it notes in places where you will see them. When God provided a vision to Habakkuk, he encouraged him with the following:

"The Lord answered me: 'Write down this vision; clearly inscribe it on tablets so one may easily read it. For the vision is yet for the appointed time; it testifies about the end and will not lie. Though it delays, wait for it, since it will certainly come and not be late.'" (Habakkuk 2:2-3 HCSB).

Don't fear. He is a good Father, and he will faithfully provide you with vision in his timing. It will not come all at once, but rather little by little, step by step, and piece by piece. Don't be discouraged by what you don't know, but be encouraged by what you do. Run with what you know while you are asking for further revelation and understanding. Write it down and keep it constantly before you, to avoid losing the vision amidst the noise and distractions.

Finally, take steps in the direction of fulfilling the vision. Do what you can today, without fretting about the bigger picture. A small step today can have big implications for your future. Just as you have learned to trust that it is God who gives vision, so trust that your actions toward the fulfillment of that vision, no matter how small, are worshipful to him and are steps of obedience in line with his plan for your life.

"All our dreams can come true, if we have
the courage to pursue them"

(Walt Disney).

CHAPTER 8

Courage Matters

In spring 2016, my sister, Cindy, began to lose the use of her arms. This started gradually when her arms tired while doing her hair. Cindy was a teacher and would get up and out of the house early each morning, as most teachers do. Because she lived with my mom, on really bad days, she would ask Mom to assist her in getting ready. Mom would help comb her hair, or assist in pulling up her slacks. Cindy pursued medical care in her search to discover what was going on. She had various blood tests, MRIs, CAT scans, and evaluations of various kinds. All tests came back negative.

Cindy had already lived with her share of trauma. Over twenty years earlier, she had almost died due to ulcerative colitis. In recent years, her marriage of over thirty years ended in divorce. Most recently, in 2015, her oldest son died after a short battle with amyotrophic lateral sclerosis (ALS). Because of these difficulties, our family had encouraged Cindy to receive counseling, hoping that what was manifesting in her body could actually be a result of post-traumatic stress or some similar disorder.

Cindy followed our encouragement and was diagnosed with PTSD. We took solace in the diagnosis and hoped that she was on the road to recovery. Further into her counseling, one of the professionals suggested that she might have "conversion disorder." Mayo Clinic defines conversion disorder as a condition in which the patient shows psychological stress in physical ways. This diagnosis also made sense to those of us who know and love Cindy.

As Cindy continued to search for answers both through counseling and medicine, by late summer one of the doctors suggested she might have ALS. When we heard the diagnosis, we were stunned. Surely the same cruel disease that took her son Dan's life the previous year couldn't now be threatening Cindy. No one in our family was prepared to consider such a devastating possibility. Days after Cindy shared the doctor's diagnosis with me, I went for a run to get some exercise and to burn off some steam.

I have a few playlists on my phone that I listen to when I run. I wasn't long into the run when "Walk On" by U2 began to play. I remember chanting along with Bono the opening lines to this song about endurance:

> And love is not the easy thing
> The only baggage that you can bring
> Is all that you can't leave behind

As I spoke the words, I began to weep, and I couldn't stop. The clash of truth in the words against the force of our circumstances broke me. As the words continued, I realized that my family was tasked with this very thing: to "walk on."

We don't get to choose what comes our way, but we do get to choose how to respond, and this requires courage. Weeks later, in mid-September, Cindy received a second opinion confirming the diagnosis. We were devastated. Yet we, along with Cindy, had to muster every bit of courage we had to walk on amidst our despair and the hopeless diagnosis until the end. What else could we do?

We are all confronted with hardship, darkness, and difficulty. Some hardships carry devastating consequences, like a difficult diagnosis, the death of a loved one, or the end of a marriage. If you haven't encountered such hardship, odds are, you will. It is part of the human condition and our shared experience on this planet. Much is required of us at such times, and chief among them is courage.

Courage is not being unafraid. Courage is being scared to death while facing your fears headlong. It is not giving up; it is fighting to the end and surrendering the result to God. I have heard it said that, in all of Scripture, the most common admonition is "fear not," and the most common refrain of Jesus is "don't be afraid." Maybe the reason is that fear confronts us regularly, an almost daily assault. And fear comes in many forms . . .

fear of harm

fear of death

fear of disease

fear of suffering

fear of what others may say or think

fear of failure

fear of success

fear of lack

fear of loss

The list goes on. Fears can be legitimate and illegitimate, rational and irrational.

My wife had a bad experience in high school where the car she was in was run off the road and totaled by an eighteen-wheeler. Since that encounter, she has battled fear every time she encounters a large truck on the highway. Others, after encountering a home invasion or crime, deal with fear related to those experiences. Even others fear danger lurking around every corner where none is present and spend their lives on pins and needles. I had an unhealthy fear of what others thought of me in early adulthood. In my senior year of college, I remember a friend letting our class know it was my birthday and the class singing happy birthday to me. For some reason, the focus and attention made me blush so much that I could feel the pulse in my face.

Since we're all going to encounter fears, difficulty, and hardship, we need courage. It is vital to our lives. So how do we embrace courage?

And what can we do to build and foster it and the holy admonition from Scripture to "fear not"?

We Are Not Alone

It helps to know and remember that we are not alone. We don't suffer in isolation and aren't the only ones who have faced insurmountable odds and unforeseen devastation and loss. It is not just that misery loves company, it's that suffering is part of the mystery of life. Partaking in this mystery strengthens our bonds with humanity. Since it is our shared narrative, it offers the opportunity to foster compassion and empathy. If properly handled, the very suffering that was meant to destroy us can instead strengthen and empower us. The same painful experience planted in the soil of our journey can yield either bitterness and hatred or love and compassion.

We need to remember and recount the stories of those now around us and those who have gone before us who lived courageously, facing their fears. Courageous stories are the best kind. They are the ones that stir our blood and inspire our hearts. They help us to navigate our own stories and make sense of them. And for our stories that never come together and of which we can never make sense, and they are many, others' stories of courage and endurance give us fuel for the mysterious journey of the unknown.

Scripture is replete with such stories. There is the story of a young shepherd boy whose nation was at war. In approaching the field of battle to bring supplies to his brothers, he assessed the situation between the battling countries and the fear paralyzing his own, and he realized that what was required was courage. Still a boy, he was unfit for battle yet was willing to risk his life for the sake of his countrymen. He had some skills, but they were unconventional and woefully modest for such an occasion. The available military weapons were ill-suited to his size and his preparation.

Mustering the courage that he had, he walked onto the battlefield and faced a hardened professional soldier who happened to be a literal giant of a man. And while David carried nothing but his courage, a sling, and five stones, Goliath was equipped from head to toe with a sword, spear, and shield in addition to his protective armor. The courageous shepherd boy won a mighty battle for himself and his nation that day. His story still speaks, inspiring people ill-equipped for battle to approach those battle-fields anyway and fight with what they have. Many battles have been won through the years because of David's example of courage.

This is one of the greatest stories of courage in all of history. But there are others. There is the story of a man of unusual strength. Samson, who courageously battled his enemies, once killed a thousand men with only the jawbone of a donkey. Obviously, an animal bone is unsuitable weaponry for warfare. Yet, with great courage, great things can happen—even the miraculous.

During another time of oppression in Israel, a young nondescript man named Gideon was privately conducting his affairs, attempting to avoid attention from his enemies. God approached him and called him to the mighty task of delivering his nation. Gideon, knowing the weight of the task, couldn't imagine a scenario where he could accomplish this. Nevertheless, the call persisted, and what was required was courage. Gideon expressed his objection and concerns to God.

"The Lord turned to him and said, 'Go in the strength you have and save Israel out of Midian's hand. Am I not sending you?' 'Pardon me, my lord,' Gideon replied, 'but how can I save Israel? My clan is the weakest in Manasseh, and I am the least in my family.' The Lord answered, 'I will be with you, and you will strike down all the Midianites, leaving none alive'" (Judges 6:14-16).

In subsequent verses, to increase his faith and courage, Gideon asked God for signs that all would go well. God willingly complied and came to the aid of his chosen one. This was particularly necessary, since God was about to ask Gideon to whittle down the army he had summoned from thirty-two thousand men to only three hundred. These odds and the call to fight made absolutely no sense in any scenario. And because of that, God knew Gideon would need additional help.

Scripture describes the armies that Gideon was about to face as being as thick as locusts. It says their camels could no more be counted than the sand on the seashore (see Judges 7:12). I'm unsure of the total number Gideon's army faced, but one reference describes one hundred twenty thousand swordsmen perishing (see Judges 8:10). Three hundred to one hundred twenty thousand? And then came the battle. The three hundred broke into three companies of one hundred each. With torches and trumpets they launched an attack on their immeasurable foe. I can't even imagine what those three hundred men were feeling. And yet, God routed the enemy who fought and struck one another instead of Gideon's men until their entire army was wiped out.

Then Gideon and his army of three hundred called on their brothers and countrymen to pursue the fleeing enemy, and together they conquered every last one. Courage and the call of God overcame unbelievable odds and won the day. However, the battle would have been lost if Gideon had not mustered courage in the face of the odds stacked against him. He went in the strength that he had and won the battle.

The nation of Israel itself is a study in courage. From such a tiny nation, we have received a wealth of lessons. At another juncture in Israel's history, the nation was again at an impasse, lined up in battle against their enemies. King Saul's son Jonathan decided to take his armor-bearer and go pick a fight against twenty or more warriors. Scripture states that in Jonathan's attack, he and his companion killed twenty men in an area of about a half acre (see 1 Samuel 14:14). This small act of courage erupted into a tumult against the armies of the Philistines who were defeated that day.

Moses, an Israelite who had been adopted and raised in Pharaoh's house as a prince of Egypt, returned to his former home after forty years in exile with a call of God for a courageous mission. The mission again seemed impossible—to deliver the Israelites from Egypt and return them to their native home. The challenge was that Egypt was one of the most powerful nations on earth and relied on the servitude of the Israelites. However, Moses embraced the call of God with courage and, through much difficulty and endurance, saw the deliverance of God.

There is the story of Esther, the Jewish queen of a Persian king, who under a death threat to all the Jews in Persia, interceded for her people and, at great risk to her own life, approached the king unannounced to request his favor. God had provided great leadership and encouragement to Esther through her uncle Mordecai. He encouraged her with this great statement of faith and courage:

> *"Mordecai told the messenger to reply to Esther,*
> *'Don't think that you will escape the fate of all the Jews*
> *because you are in the king's palace. If you keep silent*
> *at this time, liberation and deliverance will come*
> *to the Jewish people from another place, but you*
> *and your father's house will be destroyed. Who knows,*
> *perhaps you have come to your royal position*
> *for such a time as this'"* (Esther 4:13-14 HCSB).

That is how courage goes. There are no guarantees; we may live, or we may die. But what if your action and your courage is the very act that turns the tide and wins the day?

When Daniel continued to pray despite the king's edict to the contrary, he was thrown overnight into a den of ravenous lions. Daniel spent the night unharmed. The next morning, the king was so overwhelmed by Daniel's courage and his deliverance that he demanded allegiance and worship to the God of Daniel.

*"I issue a decree that in all my royal dominion, people must
tremble in fear before the God of Daniel: For He is the living God,
and He endures forever; His kingdom will never be destroyed,
and His dominion has no end. He rescues and delivers;
He performs signs and wonders in the heavens and on the earth,
for He has rescued Daniel from the power of the lions"*
(Daniel 6:26-27 HCSB).

And the following verse states that Daniel prospered during the reign of King Darius and that of his successor, King Cyrus. And by the way, those who opposed Daniel were thrown into the pit of lions and devoured. Courage saved the day.

In this same Persian empire, the Israelite sons, Shadrach, Meshach, and Abednego, refused to bow in worship to the king's idol. Their refusal incensed the king and sent him into a rage, particularly regarding their statement of faith and courage.

*"If the God we serve exists, then He can rescue us from
the furnace of blazing fire, and He can rescue us from the
power of you, the king. But even if He does not rescue us, we
want you as king to know that we will not serve your gods or
worship the gold statue you set up"* (Daniel 3:17-18 HCSB).

The king was so enraged that he demanded the furnace he made for dissenters be heated seven times hotter than normal. He then ordered some of his strongest soldiers to throw the Israelite sons into the furnace. By this time, the furnace was so hot that the flames killed those who escorted the prisoners. As the king looked into the furnace, he saw Shadrach, Meshach, and Abednego walking unharmed amidst the flames and a fourth individual who looked like a god. The king called to the prisoners to come out of the furnace, and there was not so much as the smell of smoke on them. Because of their great courage and this great deliverance of God, the king made the following proclamation:

'Praise to the God of Shadrach, Meshach, and Abednego! He sent His angel and rescued His servants who trusted in Him. They violated the king's command and risked their lives rather than serve or worship any god except their own God. Therefore I issue a decree that anyone of any people, nation, or language who says anything offensive against the God of Shadrach, Meshach, and Abednego will be torn limb from limb and his house made a garbage dump. For there is no other god who is able to deliver like this.' Then the king rewarded Shadrach, Meshach, and Abednego in the province of Babylon. (Daniel 3:28-30 HCSB)

What a turnaround started by an act of courage!

Many of our stories have happy endings such as these. Yet many don't. Acts of courage can lead to great turnarounds, but this is not always the case, and there are no guarantees. John the Baptist was beheaded at the whim of Herod. Jesus, the sinless Son of God, was crucified though He had committed no crime. Dietrich Bonhoeffer was executed in a German prison just days before the camp's liberation. In Hebrews 11, the writer spends the chapter describing heroes of the faith, many who accomplished great things and others who did not.

And what more can I say? Time is too short for me to tell about Gideon, Barak, Samson, Jephthah, David, Samuel, and the prophets, who by faith conquered kingdoms, administered justice, obtained promises, shut the mouths of lions, quenched the raging of fire, escaped the edge of the sword, gained strength after being weak, became mighty in battle, and put foreign armies to flight. Women received their dead—they were raised to life again. Some men were tortured, not accepting release, so that they might gain a better resurrection, and others experienced mockings and scourgings, as well as bonds and imprisonment. They were stoned, they were sawed in two, they died by the sword, they wandered about in sheepskins, in goatskins, destitute, afflicted, and mistreated. The world was not worthy of them. They wandered in deserts and on mountains, hiding in caves and holes in the ground. All these were approved through their faith, but they did not receive what was promised, since God had provided something better for us, so that they would not be made perfect without us. (Hebrews 11:32-40 HCSB)

"The world was not worthy of them" describes men and women of faith and courage. They see differently and have a different focus. Here in Hebrews 11, we find a description of this difference. In describing Moses, the text says this:

"By faith Moses, when he had grown up, refused to be called
the son of Pharaoh's daughter and chose to suffer with the
people of God rather than to enjoy the short-lived pleasure of sin.
For he considered the reproach because of the Messiah
to be greater wealth than the treasures of Egypt, since
his attention was on the reward. By faith he left Egypt behind,
not being afraid of the king's anger, for Moses persevered as one
who sees Him who is invisible" (Hebrews 11:24-27 HCSB).

Moses had courage to live differently because he valued different things, his focus was different, and he was looking for a different treasure than the treasures of this world. From his courage and the courage of all the heroic individuals who lived before us and who live among us now, we draw inspiration to feed our hearts and stir courage for our journeys.

"Therefore, since we also have such a large cloud of witnesses
surrounding us, let us lay aside every weight and the sin that so
easily ensnares us. Let us run with endurance the race that lies
before us, keeping our eyes on Jesus, the source and perfecter

*of our faith, who for the joy that lay before Him endured a cross
and despised the shame and has sat down at the right hand of
God's throne. For consider Him who endured such hostility
from sinners against Himself, so that you won't grow
weary and lose heart"* (Hebrews 12:1-3 HCSB).

Trouble

The beginning of courage is trouble. Without trouble or hardship, courage remains unnecessary, unexercised, and unused. I don't celebrate trouble and don't look forward to its visit. However, only when it appears do I have the opportunity to exercise and grow courage. For some, trouble seems a companion all too constant. Maybe these folks are the most courageous among us.

When trouble makes its rounds, we have a choice. We can choose fear or courage. As our first response, I suggest we make trouble a call to prayer. The friend of Job was correct when he made the following assessment:

*"But mankind is born for trouble as surely as sparks fly upward.
However, if I were you, I would appeal to
God and would present my case to Him.
He does great and unsearchable things,
wonders without number"* (Job 5:7-9 HCSB).

Many of life's experiences are beyond our pay grade to understand, including trouble and suffering. Thankfully, for all the things we don't know, we do know some. One of those is that God is compassionate and loving. Another is his invitation for us to call out to him in prayer and to bring our troubles before him. Prayer in and of itself is a mystery, but we know that God is pleased with it, is moved by it, and responds to it. He answers prayer. We may not like and understand his answers, but he does respond. So, by our prayer, we have an opportunity to ask our loving and compassionate God for aid and comfort in our trouble and for deliverance and victory from our trouble. You have heard the phrase, "If you don't ask, you'll never know" or "If you don't ask, you'll never have." Petition God with your request, present your case before him, and ask him to intervene in your trouble and suffering.

Perhaps

Perhaps he will intervene and deliver. Perhaps he will reverse the present course. Perhaps he will send aid from afar—compassionate care, resources, or whatever it is that you need. Perhaps he will deliver again as he did with Daniel, Esther, and Shadrach, Meshach, and Abednego when they bowed their knees and prayed and petitioned for God's help. You will never know if you don't ask.

As I was reading Scripture recently and praying over what I read, I realized how my experiences and circumstances have led me to doubt his faithfulness and to doubt that he will answer my prayers. In Job 33, the youngest of Job's friends rebukes Job for his complaining and refutes his complaint.

> *"But I tell you, in this you are not right, for God is greater than any mortal. Why do you complain to him that he responds to no one's word?" (Job 33:12-13).*

Those words pierced my heart, and I realized that though I don't voice my complaint out loud, in my heart I have judged God due to the volume of my unanswered prayers. Without question, this has led to prayerlessness in my life. I still believe in God. I believe he loves me and gave Jesus as a sacrifice for my sins. I still believe in heaven. Even so, like Mary and Martha, the weight of my personal pain falls heavy on me.

I don't understand God's delay or his response, which I interpret as his absence. I find myself accusing Jesus of not caring, of not showing up when I need him the most. I may not verbalize it, but it weighs heavy on my heart. And if I'm not careful, it leads me to go through the motions of asking with little hope or belief that he will intervene; either that, or it leads me to quit asking altogether. And herein lies the invitation to courage.

Perhaps. Perhaps he will intervene again. Perhaps as in the case of so many others, he will step into the midst of horrible circumstances and unbelievable odds, and act. Perhaps he will grant my request and your request. I take hope and courage in that he has invited his people to ask throughout history. I take hope and courage in that he has intervened in the past. I think part of our struggle as Americans is that we interpret our lives through a lens of entitlement. We expect good, we expect blessing, and we expect favor, and we misinterpret the circumstances of our lives that seem to contradict those. When I study the accounts of courageous heroes of the Bible, they seemed to live with abandonment. This was reflected in their expectations of the circumstances they faced. Esther fasted and prayed for three days, asking God for favor before risking her life appealing to the king. Yet she was willing to risk it, unsure of what might follow. As her uncle Mordecai exclaimed, *"Perhaps you have come to your royal position for such a time as this"* (Esther 4:14 CSB). And Shadrach, Meshach, and Abednego, all Hebrew men of prayer, risked their lives by refusing to bow to the Babylonian idol, and with abandon stated, *"He can rescue us from the power of you, the king. But even if He does not rescue us, . . . we will not . . . worship the gold statue you set up"* (Daniel 3:17-18 HCSB).

What courageous abandonment to God! I encourage you, that though you don't understand your circumstances nor can fully interpret the events of your life, to present your requests to God, to pour out your complaints to him, and to ask for his goodness, his compassion, and his intervention. He encourages us to do that. He has intervened throughout history. Perhaps he will intervene again. You will only know if you have the courage to ask and then abandon yourself to him.

Perfect Love

Abandoning yourself to anything is never easy. Abandonment has to do with relinquishing control, with yielding and giving up your rights and expectations. The only way to effectively abandon yourself is to trust and believe in the object of your abandon. The reason we can abandon ourselves to God is that God is love. The more we grow in love—the more we understand, believe, and participate in it—the stronger we become in our faith and courage. If we truly believe he loves us—really loves us—we can abandon ourselves to him. I suggest, if you are struggling to trust God in your current circumstances and are consequently unable to abandon yourself to him, you should press into his love for you more and more.

What does that mean? I encourage you to consider God's love expressed throughout Scripture and fully demonstrated in Jesus. Read about it, meditate on it, and pray about it, asking the Father to reveal it to your heart. Scripture says, *"Perfect love casts out fear"* (1 John 4:18 NKJV), and I believe the more we understand his love, the more we can abandon ourselves to him. Ask God to reveal his love to your heart by his Holy Spirit. Romans 5:5 states that the Holy Spirit is responsible for this. If your love is at a low ebb, ask the Lord about that, ask him to reveal more of his love to you by the Holy Spirit, and see if you can mine its height, depth, width, and breadth. Set your heart on him and his love for you, see if you can seek and discover another dimension that may have escaped you in the past, and watch the flame of your courage begin to grow. Love is a weapon against fear. Pursue love and reap a harvest of courage.

Finally, as you grow in love and grow in courage, remember you are not alone. Trouble is the lot of every man. Remember the stories of those before you and those around you who with great courage faced their troubles. Look for God in every circumstance, and make trouble a call to prayer. Take hope and courage that God loves and knows you and that perhaps he will intervene and deliver as he has done before and will do again. And though the difficulty is beyond your pay grade to know or understand, know that your courage will be greatly rewarded. Whether you are delivered or whether you die in faith, you will have lived a courageous life. You will have embraced the words of Jesus to be unafraid, and you will have taken your place among the heroes.

CHAPTER 9

Authenticity Matters

Growing up, we all role-play. I remember dressing up as Uncle Sam for a kindergarten production. In first grade, I was Little Boy Blue. On the elementary playground, I was Detective Steve McGarrett from Hawaii Five-O. At baseball practice, I was Brooks Robinson at third base. During my middle school years, shooting baskets I was Pistol Pete Maravich, and playing football I was Larry Csonka. We all dream of whom we could be and strive to become like those we admire.

There is a time for emulating others. As we mature, our goal is to move closer to our authentic selves and become who God created us to be. As Søren Kierkegaard said, "Now, with God's help, I shall become myself." Part of maturity occurs naturally with the passing of time, but not fully. It also happens as we choose maturity over immaturity. As Saint Paul wrote, *"When I was a child, I talked like a child, I thought like a child, I reasoned like a child. When I became a man, I put the ways of childhood behind me"* (1 Corinthians 13:11).

On the path to authenticity, we try on many roles and identities as we look for our true selves. Just as I role-played, I witnessed the same things in my kids. As they grew socially and developed friendships, I noticed that they would pick up the mannerisms of others. In addition to dressing like their friends, they would even pick up ways of talking and acting like them. As they have matured, they have begun to settle into their own unique identities, and I couldn't be prouder of them as individuals.

It takes courage to be our true selves. It's a risk to let the world see you and me. If it rejects a false self, that's not a big deal. However, if it sees the real you and offers rejection, that's different. Yet God made only one you. Psalm 139 says you are "fearfully and wonderfully made." Only one individual has your DNA and your fingerprints. Since there will never be another you in the world, why not be the best you that you can be while you are here? As Judy Garland said, "Always be a first-rate version of yourself, instead of a second-rate version of someone else."

Comparison

> Use what talents you possess; the woods would be very silent
> if no birds sang there except those that sang best.
>
> —Henry Van Dyke

It's important to be yourself no matter the cost. If you and I are not careful, we can judge our gifts and contributions as insignificant, particularly in comparison with someone else's who we judge to be superior. That's why comparison is such a trap. The world needs all of us. Just because I don't have the voice of James Taylor doesn't mean I shouldn't sing.

As a businessman, I can view my career with satisfaction. However, if I choose to compare myself with others more successful, I can begin to look at my accomplishments in a less favorable light. Taking it a step further, if I compare myself with Bill Gates, Sam Walton, or Howard Schultz, my business life might seem like a complete failure.

The truth is that I don't know the stories or struggles of any of these men. Even if I did, I'm not responsible for them. I will not be judged by my accomplishments or stewardship in comparison to anyone. I will only be judged by what I did or didn't do with what I was given. How did I steward the gifts and talents that were invested in me? If I attempt to be Howard Schultz, I am not being myself.

"I do not try to dance better than anyone else.
I only try to dance better than myself"
(Mikhail Baryshnikov, ballet dancer).

Authentic versus Phony

You might as well be the real you because everyone can smell a phony. Some phonies can hide it for a while, but eventually, people will know. It's exhausting to put on a mask that doesn't fit and to walk in someone else's shoes. Why not drop the facade and fully enter into the life you were meant to live?

At times you will be rejected and heartbroken. Still, living the life you were meant to live will be freeing, freeing you from the expectations of others and freeing you to be yourself. You can settle into your own soul, wear your own clothes, and walk in your own shoes. This is your call and destiny.

The Builder and the Architect

Because of freedom and opportunity, many say we can be anything we want. That may be true, as I know many talented people who can do many things well. Others are gifted in one specific thing.

Years ago I heard an analogy about life that has proven useful. The analogy compared the living of our lives to the construction of a building. Before the project begins, it's important for the builder to meet the architect to discuss the project at hand. The builder receives the plans and reviews them thoroughly. After their initial meeting, it's best for the builder to consult the architect throughout the project to ensure a thorough understanding of each aspect of the plan. As the project advances and challenges are encountered, such meetings allow design elements to be added and changes to be made.

Since God is our creator and the architect of our lives, isn't it wise to regularly consult him about who we become and how we live the life he has given us? It's fitting that we should prayerfully live our lives before God, asking for his daily guidance and the unveiling of his plans. His plan will come into view as we spend time with him.

One of my favorite passages of Scripture states, *"Unless the Lord builds the house, the builders labor in vain. Unless the Lord watches over the city, the guards stand watch in vain"* (Psalm 127:1). Paul, writing to the Corinthians, declares, *"You are God's field, God's building"* (1 Corinthians 3:9). I don't want to build and pursue a life of my own choosing when the God who created me has other plans. I want to consult with him and follow his lead. Whether you have many talents or one, I encourage you to go to God and ask him what he had in mind when he made you. Then set yourself to do it with all your heart, soul, mind, and strength. And don't forget to consult him regularly, as he may have some additions or changes as you build.

Sure, you can go your own way and pursue what you want. You can chase whatever crosses your path or catches your eye, whether money, power, fame, or success. God is crazy about you and longs for you to be fulfilled in the fullness of your heart. And he will be cheering for you! Only, he created you on purpose for a purpose. What better place to start than with your creator, asking what he has for you, asking why he created you, and asking how you can steward your life to become all he desires you to be.

The Journey

Like most of life, becoming authentic is a journey rather than a destination. We don't choose it once and then walk in authenticity from that point forward. Instead, we continue to move in that direction with every decision and choice we make. We will continually be pressed upon to choose the easier path of the false self, consisting of posing, comparison, and pride. Keep in mind, we should choose the better path of transparency and humility. It is more difficult but offers more life and power than the false self could ever hope to muster.

Christian circles, however well intentioned, have harmed us with their excessive emphasis on the triumphant victorious life. It sounds good, but it is not the life of our shared humanity. Because real life is so different from this ideal, it can lead to posing rather than authenticity.

The victorious Christian life espoused by Jesus wasn't a get-rich-quick scheme or one removed from difficulties. The early disciples encountered unending trouble just as we do today, including sickness, persecution, heartache, betrayal, accidents, injury, and death. Even then, their faith transcended their experience and infused their journey with both a gritty faith and a hope in the God who saves.

Instead of living some plastic veneer of victory, the world needs to see real victory. They need to see an overcoming life, one that despite death and loss clings to faith. One that despite betrayal chooses friendship. That despite despair clings to hope. They need to see the real us with all our bumps and bruises, clinging with tenacity and threadbare faith to the God who offers hope and help in this life, and in the next, eternal victory. It is in our brokenness, more than in our victories, that people can relate to and connect to our stories. As Leonard Cohen sang,

> Forget your perfect offering
> There is a crack in everything
> That's how the light gets in
> (Leonard Cohen, "Anthem")

This is our one and only life. Don't have a cavalier attitude, just letting life happen. Instead, steward your life and dive in with all the gusto you have. Give all your heart, soul, mind, and strength to becoming the best, most authentic person you can be.

It's interesting that people can spend more time preparing for a vacation or a weekend trip than they spend preparing for their life.

Approach life as you would for a mountain expedition. Read many books, study many maps, research many resources, and network with many people. Find sources of encouragement and inspiration. This is your one shot, so make it count!

> What is it you plan to do
> with your one wild and precious life?
> (Mary Oliver, "The Summer Day")

I encourage you to journal as a way of paying attention. Journaling has helped me to listen to my life and to document the discoveries made along the way. I've kept boxes of paper journals through the years. Since I regularly sit in front of a computer, I also journal online. Find out what works for you.

Additionally, I encourage you to feed your curiosity by reading and becoming a lifelong learner. I have read many helpful books about how a person can discover their true self and life purpose. A few of my favorites include these:

Abba's Child by Brennan Manning

The Echo Within by Robert Benson

Let Your Life Speak by Parker Palmer

20,000 Days and Counting by Robert D. Smith

It's Your Call by Gary Barkalow

To Be Told by Dan B. Allender, PhD

Some organizations exist to help people uncover their gifts and talents. Two that have been very helpful for me are Your One Degree (www.yourone-degree.com) and Polished Arrows International (www.polishedarrows.org).

I wish I had more to offer. Yet, this journey is one for which you alone bear responsibility. I'm not saying you're isolated or must travel alone. What I am saying is that you bear the weight for your life—your choices, decisions, and actions. The good news is that we can walk in community with others and find help along the way. Get all the help you can.

CHAPTER 10

Love Matters

Nothing is more important than love. If ever there was a universally accepted idea, it is this. Things that are true are universally true, so if they're true in the church, they're true in the world. Love is the ultimate truth. We see it in young love, and we see it in marriages lasting decades. We see it in a young husband and wife welcoming a newborn child into their family. And we see it in middle-aged moms and dads launching young adult children into lives of their own.

We see it in heartfelt friendships lasting decades. And we see it in soldiers willing to fight to protect their homeland and the ones they love. We see it in actions great and small. Our greatest songs are love songs, and our greatest stories are love stories. Our deepest emotions and longings deal with love. Some have misguided notions and understandings of love, but love remains central.

Nearing the end of his letter to the Roman Christians, the apostle Paul lists some of God's commands and then states, *"Whatever other command there may be, are summed up in this one command: 'Love your neighbor as yourself.' Love does no harm to a neighbor. Therefore love is the fulfillment of the law"* (Romans 13:9-10). Paul is echoing the words of Jesus. When Jesus was asked what the greatest commandment is, he responded by saying the greatest is to love God with all your heart, soul, mind, and strength and the second greatest is to love your neighbor as yourself (see Matthew 22:36-39; Mark 12:28-31; Luke 10:27-28). He went on to stress the supremacy of love by saying, *"All the Law and the Prophets hang on these two commandments"* (Matthew 22:40).

My heart is set on God, I know this to be true. I desire to know him and for him to be proud of me. I desire to honor him with the life I live and the choices I make. I also know that I fail almost every day in my love and affection for him. Mercifully, the more I know him, the more I realize his love is not predicated on my performance. I sense him cheering for me and encouraging me despite my feeble efforts.

God is easy to love; the rest of the human race, not so much. Maybe one of the reasons we struggle loving others is that we struggle loving ourselves. After spending most of his adult life traveling the world as a self-proclaimed vagabond evangelist, Brennan Manning observed that self-hatred was the predominant spiritual problem with which he dealt. That is a staggering statement, but all too believable. However, as you and I encounter the goodness of God day by day and begin to believe we are loved, maybe we can begin to apply that same love to ourselves and others. Only once we have received love can we truly give love.

God Is Love

As a Christian, I believe that the origin of all things is found in God, and so it is with love. Love is the story that God is telling throughout history.

We could define God in many ways and attempt to list all his attributes. Scripture does as much, providing names and attributes to help in our understanding of who he is. Some of those include Jehovah, Most High, Almighty, Incomparable, Omnipotent, Sovereign and Everlasting. The most complete and clarifying definition provided is also the simplest: God is love. The disciple who knew Jesus best said as much: *"Whoever does not love does not know God, because God is love"* (1 John 4:8).

I am not a poet, but a few years ago I was searching for a way to express the love that I have encountered in God, and this is the result.

Love.

It is your atmosphere.

It is the aura that surrounds you.

It is your essence, the essence of who you are.

It defines you and yet it can't be defined.

It is everlasting and boundless.

It cannot be measured.

It is beyond description.

It is the best thing about you.

It is the best thing about life.

The cream of the crop.

Love.

Love is alive.

Love is.

It exists.

We can pursue it.

We can walk away from it.

We can go its direction, or we can go the other direction.

We can participate in it.

We can join in or stay on the outside.

It sounds too good to be true.

Surrounding us is hardness and hate.

Yet there is love.

The hardness and hate do not diminish love.

When I drink from the cup of love, I am satisfied.

When I taste and see, I realize it is good.

God is love.

God is good.

The boredom of life, the tedium and monotony

do not diminish it.

It may feel diminished, it may seem minimized, but it is not.

It is not.

Love is alive.

Even in death, love lives.

Even in pain, love exists.

Love longs for you.

Love longs for me.

Love is calling.

Love is pursuing.

Love is crying aloud.

Love is stronger, not weaker.

Love still sings.

Love still resounds and echoes.

Love was and is declared and continues to unfold.

There is more revelation of God's love today

than ever before.

Testimony after testimony of the love of God.

Sharing Love

Before the creation of the world, God existed as a family in community together—Father, Son, and Holy Spirit—known as the Trinity, one God demonstrated and expressed in three persons or personalities. His love was so expansive that he wanted to express it further. As a result, he created us so he could share his love.

Union

Love seeks union, someone with whom to share it. Jesus said as much when he stated, *"I have given them the glory you gave to me, that they may be one as we are one. With me in them and you in me, may they be so perfected in unity that the world will recognize that it was you who sent me and that you have loved them as you have loved me"* (John 17:22-23 NJB).

How amazing is that! This God who longs to share his love sent his son to win our hearts, inviting us into union. And not only that, Romans 5:5 says that God also sent his Holy Spirit to pour out his love into our hearts. This gift is not dependent on our efforts.

Love within Marriage

The greatest opportunity we have on earth to enter into the mystery of union is through the covenant of marriage. This is why marriage is so important; so very important that God's Holy Word both begins and ends in marriage—Adam and Eve's in Genesis, and Jesus and his church in Revelation. Marriage is the foundation of family and the bedrock of society. Without a father and mother, there is no family or children. Where there are no children, the family line comes to an end.

Since God invented marriage, then those who enter it should make every effort to understand and submit to his purposes for it. This is particularly true for those of us who follow him. God commanded husbands to love their wives just as Christ loved the church and laid down his life for her (see Ephesians 5:25). You may say, "Wow! No way. That is too hard and too much to ask." So is anything worth fighting for. Why would you expect marriage to be any different?

Since God created marriage, I believe his enemies are hellishly fighting against it. We see this opposition prominently on display in our culture.

My marriage to Carrie is one of the great blessings of my life. Many blessings exist in my life, and many things matter to me. Of all of them, including family and friends, health and financial stability, none has higher importance than my marriage to her.

I know that I take Carrie for granted, as I do with most blessings in life. I don't want to do that. I want to honor and cherish our time together. She is the finest human being I have ever met and is my closest friend. She knows everything about me and still loves me. This is what union is meant to be.

Others are not as fortunate as Carrie and I are, as we see marriages in tatters all around us. The destruction caused by them is tragic, affecting every area: relationships, faith, finances, mental health, family life, and social standing. Our hearts break for friends and family as they live among the ashes and strive to build a new normal in the aftermath of ruined marriages.

Brokenness, infidelity, and divorce all happen, but they are not God's best. If they happen, look to God, knowing that he can bring beauty from ashes and put broken pieces back together again. By all means don't remain discouraged, and whatever you do, don't give up. God is always loving and cheering us on.

Love within Family

I am grateful for a loving mom and dad. Mom and Dad shared a tremendous love that extended over fifty years. It carried them through both good times and bad. It strengthened Mom as she cared so beautifully for Dad over the final decade of his life. Their love provided a great example of what marriage could be. I have seen that love echo in the lives of my brother and sister and in their marriages and families. It also influences mine, and I'm hopeful of its passing further to the generations to come.

I love my family, my wife, and my children. I long for the best for them; for happiness, success, and for the deepest longings of their hearts to come true. I long for them to know God in meaningful and intimate ways.

I long for them to be bold and courageous and to live life unafraid, to give it their all and to do their very best. I hope they will not be sidetracked and derailed along the journey of life, and I hope they will not encounter too much brokenness and heartache. Yet I also know that heartache and brokenness are inevitable and that therein lie some of life's best lessons. I wish for their hearts to be strong and true, filled with love and hope.

To receive love is the greatest of gifts. God started the idea of giving, and I have benefited immensely from his love. I stumble around, imperfectly offering my love to others. And what a blessing when love returns!

Carrie and I have enjoyed every season we have had with our kids. It is not that the seasons have been without challenge or difficulty, but we love Luke and Kellie and they have our hearts. We love being with them and would give anything for them, and we do. We provide for them and help them. We adventure with them and pray for them. We offer ourselves to them in whatever way we can, including our time, our resources, our counsel, our prayers, and our hearts.

They are now young adults, living and making decisions on their own. But Luke and Kellie know that wherever Carrie and I are, they are always welcome. Our home will always also be their home. They are our family and they are our hearts. My desire is that they would not wander far. However, if life's adventures take them far away, they will always be near in heart. And so it is with our heavenly family.

Love within Friendship

> A friend is what the heart needs all the time.
>
> —Henry Van Dyke

Friendship is one of life's great gifts, and my life is enriched because of it. I'm fortunate to be a man who has friends. In part, I attribute it to the influence of my parents who showed me the way to value and honor others. I have many friends and am grateful for each and every one of them. There are other people I meet and admire from a distance, and I know that, if given the opportunity, we could be friends.

However, the truth is that we are limited in our capacity for friendship. Though I would like to be friends to many, if I spread myself too thin, I limit my capacity to be a friend to anyone at all. Still, we can be friendly to all and carry the spirit of friendship; a spirit that welcomes and encourages, a spirit of kindness and affection.

You were born into your family, but you choose your friends. This is the power of friendship. One of my dearest friends is my friend Pete. We met two years after I graduated from college. I was working at Coopers and Lybrand, one of the eight largest accounting firms in the world, and Pete was studying accounting at Oral Roberts University like I did. He was interviewing for a job at Coopers, and I was assigned to take him to lunch.

We hit it off at lunch and discovered that we shared mutual friends. During lunch he invited me to a Bible study he and his wife Mary Kay were starting. Over the next eight years, we met most Friday nights; hanging out, drinking coffee, praying, worshipping, and studying the Bible together.

I grieved with Pete and Mary Kay as they buried their first child, and celebrated with them as they welcomed the rest of their clan into the world—Katie, Aaron and Austin. My second date with Carrie was with Pete and Mary Kay at the opera. The following spring, we all went skiing in Oregon, which Carrie and I refer to as the trip where we fell in love.

On Carrie's thirtieth birthday, we flew to Oregon to celebrate with Pete and Mary Kay. We had a ball exploring the Pacific Northwest together, a place we would further explore in recent years with Luke and Kellie. On my fortieth birthday, we again celebrated with our friends in Chicago, and on Luke's sixteenth birthday, Luke and I flew to Colorado to ski with Pete and his sons.

These are all just a sampling of time we invested in our friendship. In some seasons we have walked closer than in others. Our families have both had challenges and difficulties: thyroid and breast cancer, the loss of a child, loss of relatives, autism, job losses, a failed business, strained relationships, and difficult family dynamics. And though we have been separated by thousands of miles, we have shared in these challenges.

One thing I know is that I have a friend in Pete. He and Mary Kay believe in me and love me. They have shown their friendship through the years by their actions and their love.

The most important thing about our friendship is that we have chosen it. We have chosen to call, write, visit, and invest in each other's lives. We can't be there all the time, but we are there when we can be. I can count on Pete's friendship. I can count on Pete's birthday card every year and the Starbucks card enclosed. It has been such a privilege to have Pete as a lifelong friend.

I have been blessed with other friends as well. My dearest friends are the ones with whom I can be myself. No pretense, just friendship. Friendship really is a mutual affection and appreciation for each other.

Maybe you have had your heart broken in friendship or been betrayed by friends. So have I. This is a sad part of our human experience. Even if you have not felt such betrayal, I'm sure you have felt the pain of rejection and exclusion. Carrie has aided me immensely in dealing with such pain, as she has such a gift of forgiveness and of extending love and friendship. My natural tendency is to protect my heart and withdraw. Hers is to press ahead and offer love in spite of rejection. She has helped me to love. I believe poet Alfred Lord Tennyson's words:

> 'Tis better to have loved and lost
> Than never to have loved at all.
>
> ("In Memoriam A. H. H.")

I encourage you to choose love. In spite of its cost, there is nothing as great as love.

CHAPTER 11

Home Matters

Home means many things to many people. I had a great home. If that isn't true for you, I'm certainly sorry and don't want my thoughts here to be offensive. Yet, I can only write of what I know, what I have experienced, and what I believe to be true.

I'm one of the lucky ones who has always had a home. I grew up having a mom and dad, a brother and sister, and a place where we belonged. Growing up as a part of an air force family, we moved frequently. So home was less about the particular house than it was about the people with whom it was shared.

Dad and Mom set the tone. Dad was a man of integrity. He was tall, dark, and handsome and crazy about Mom. He was disciplined. I remember rising early in the morning throughout my life to find him exercising in the family room where he did calisthenics every day, in addition to running five times a week. He was warm and welcoming. Though he had a demanding job, he always made time for us kids. I remember playing "Tickleman," where he would tickle us until we couldn't breathe. He loved the outdoors, and he fostered that love in us through camping, waterskiing, hunting, and fishing. He didn't say much, but what he did say was always important.

Mom loved and supported us kids and Dad. She always cheered Dad on in whatever the venture. She loved and welcomed our friends, and in whatever activities we chose to pursue, she was there cheering us on. If

Dad and Mom ever had difficulties in their marriage, I didn't see it. Our home was always solid and always safe, and for that I am most grateful.

I don't want to deceive you into believing that we lived in some Pollyannaish world. That is not true. There is no perfect home, and there are no perfect people. We all are broken, and most of us are doing our best to pick up the pieces and build better lives. In my parents' case, Dad came from a home where he never saw his father rise out of bed. From his earliest memory, his dad was bedridden with crippling arthritis. Due to the stress and strain of my grandfather's condition and a lack of income to take care of my dad and his sister, my grandmother suffered with bouts of mental instability. My mom was raised by her grandparents after her parents divorced when she was just a toddler. So Mom and Dad, without ideal homes of their own, decided to build a good home for us.

As for Carrie and me, our home, though imperfect, was also a loving, accepting, and stable place. Unlike our families who lived in a multitude of homes, states, and countries over the years, our kids have only known three homes in the same city their entire lives. Still, it is not the house that makes the home, but the people with whom it is shared and what is shared among the people.

So let's discover more about what defines a home. Most definitions typically center around a person's place of residence or dwelling, and the family or people that reside together. Additional definitions include the idea of home as the center of domestic affairs. In essence, your home base. Another definition includes your place of origin with broader implications, such as a region, a country, a state, or a city. All of these provide texture and meaning to the word *home*.

A few other ideas of home resonate with me. They include the idea of home being a place of refreshment, a place of flourishing and belonging, and a place of refuge. Additionally, I particularly like the idea of home being a destination or goal, the finishing point in a race, or the place to which we are returning.

A Place of Beginnings

I'm unsure of my earliest memory of home, only that I always had one. I knew this was where I belonged and that the people there were special. We shared life together. We shared most meals together; maybe not breakfast and lunch, but surely almost every dinner. There were exceptions, like when football practice went late, or when Dad was out of town, or Cindy was spending the night with her friends, or Greg was hanging out at his girlfriend's house. But for the most part, Mom had a home-cooked meal for us every night, and we sat down together as a family and shared a meal and shared our day. We were family. Everybody had a seat, typically the same seat every night, and everybody belonged.

Decades later, Carrie and I raised our family the same way, sharing a home-cooked meal almost every night. During Luke's sixth grade year, his teacher asked for a show of hands to see how many kids in the class shared a meal with their families at least two times per week. Out of almost thirty kids in his class, only Luke and one other raised their hands. When he shared that story at dinner, we were shocked. Something so simple that was a building block of our home was being ignored by most of the families around us.

This shared meal helped foster our family identity. Everyone in the family knew they had a place at the table and that they belonged. They also knew it was a safe and welcoming place for others. All their friends were welcome at our table. Eating is a daily necessity; therefore, the shared meal is a daily opportunity to foster the idea of home. Sharing any meal is a personal and intimate act. Sharing a meal in your home is even more so. It is a welcome into your refuge and your life.

A Place of Belonging

In addition to my place at the table, I had my own bedroom and even my own place in the car. I was celebrated on birthdays and holidays, and I was supported in my activities. Whenever possible, my family came to my football games and my swim meets. My friends were important, my thoughts were important, my hurts were important, and my words were important. Belonging is fostered by all these ways. It's fostered by acceptance and embrace, participation and inclusion.

I can remember as early as first grade when we lived in Selma, Alabama, heading to the river during the warm summer evenings and on weekends. Greg, Cindy, and I all learned to ski when we were between five and seven years old. A few years later, when we moved to Prattville, we progressed from going on day trips to packing our ski boat full of camping gear and heading to nearby Lake Martin. We would camp at night, and ski and swim during the day. We camped for a few years, until we bought a cabin. During our five years in Prattville, we spent most summer weekends at the lake. Many times we were joined by friends, but we were always with our family.

I have endless memories of these times. I remember when my granddad learned to ski. It was awesome to see my sixty-eight-year-old granddad skiing for the very first time. That same trip we got caught in a terrible storm, and were soaked while huddling underneath the boat awning as we slowly made our way back to shore.

Dad taught most of our friends and family members to ski. He was a great teacher and unbelievably patient. I also remember countless games in the evenings and laughing hysterically, particularly at Dad. He was good at games. Some of my favorite memories are of us sitting inside a screened porch, watching the rain come across the lake. Maybe these times are why I love the water so much; it feels like home.

A Place of Becoming

Though I am fully accountable for who I am, much was handed down to me from my parents and family. This includes the good and the bad. For me, home included love and acceptance. For others, it included dysfunction and trauma. Either way, we all are a product of our environment, and home is the place where we begin the process of becoming.

The seeds of who we become are planted in the fertile soil of youth, in the place we call home.

Dad handed down to my siblings and me honesty and integrity. Mom handed down encouragement and support. Both handed down love; for each other, for our family, and for our fellow man. Mom and Dad treated everyone with love and respect and always, in every situation, desired to do the right thing, fully convinced that there is such a thing. I always felt hope with Mom and Dad. I always felt strength. There was always light, always faith, always hope, and always love.

They handed down some other things as well. Dad didn't cuss often, but when he got really mad, he had a "go-to phrase" that I'm sure someone handed down to him. I have introduced this phrase to my wife and kids, against my wife's best wishes and continued counsel. When I get really angry or frustrated, I can hear my dad in the sound of my own voice when I use the phrase.

As for Mom, she has some perfectionist tendencies that she saw fit to hand to me. She is also a tireless worker and doer and will not rest until whatever is on her mind is done. These can be good traits, but they also have consequences. I inherited these traits from my mom, and my family and friends have borne the consequences, good and bad.

I become who I am because of what gets handed down to me and, ultimately, what I choose to do with what I've received. I like an analogy that a former pastor of mine used. He said that we are responsible for acting as traffic police in our lives. The things handed down that we want to keep we should allow to pass. However, for the things we desire to end, we should hold up a stop sign and say, "This far and no further; it ends here." Embrace the good, and throw out the bad. Don't despise the bad, or regret it. Learn from it, and choose how you will live and what you will pass on.

A Place of Wrestling

This place of becoming means we wrestle with who we want or do not want to become. We try different things on for size to see if they fit and how they wear. We take them out on test drives to see how they work and if they ring true. This pertains to things handed down from our parents and also from God. It became clear when my siblings and I all got married and started having kids that each child was uniquely made and wildly different. Early on, before we had a chance to influence them, each had a personality of their own.

This wrestling includes many choices, things to reject and things to embrace. And these choices are never easy. Sometimes rejecting things handed down to us from our parents seems to be a rejection of our parents. It isn't, but it feels that way. Some of the things God has placed within us get buried along the way, so we lose sight of them. They may lie dormant for years, only to be stumbled upon later down the road. So we wrestle, we stumble, and we fight.

Life is a participation sport not intended for spectators. At least that is true for those who live well. If you don't wrestle, stumble, and fight for who you are and who you want to be, you will never become the wonderfully unique expression of God that he intends for you to be. It is much like the transformation of a caterpillar into a beautiful butterfly. The caterpillar must dig its way out of the cocoon to become a butterfly and begin to fly.

A Place of Faith

Home is also the place where our faith begins. I'm unsure of my first memory of church. It was either at a church one of my grandmothers attended in Kentucky, or it was when Mom bribed me to go to Easter service with her. Actually, I was the one who did the bribing. I was in third grade at the time, and we were living on the air force base in Selma, Alabama. The Osmond Brothers had just become an instant hit with the release of their first album and their first hit "One Bad Apple." I liked the song and wanted the album, so when Mom asked me to go to church, I told her I would join her if she bought me the new album. She did, and so began my early memories of church.

A few years later, Mom and Dad informed us that we were going to start attending the little Methodist church in our neighborhood. Mom and Dad had both grown up Methodist, so when they decided to return to church, this seemed like the place to start. We began regularly attending, and we all really liked it. We liked the pastor and the people, we liked the hymns of faith, and we liked learning about God. It wasn't long before we all grew to love the church. More importantly, we learned to love the God of the church. This was the true beginning of my faith journey.

The journey has taken me many places, places too numerous to count. It has included regular Sunday worship from those early days to now. It has included youth groups, youth choirs, summer camps, and hundreds of retreats. It has included decisions about which college I attended, activities I chose, and jobs I accepted. I have gone on mission trips, and have given much of my life, energy, and resources to the building of God's family in and through the local churches where I have worshipped. My faith in God has been the center of my marriage, the center of my family, and the center of my life. And it all began at home. Home truly is a place of faith.

A Place You Leave

My grandparents lived in the same houses their entire adult lives. Going to visit them was a special treat. Those houses were filled with sights and smells that bring back a flood of memories. At 515 Ford Avenue where my Grandmother Kittinger lived, my siblings and I spent hours playing in all its old nooks and crannies. It was a two-story house with a full basement. As a kid, the house seemed huge. At the top of the stairs were three small doors for attic storage. Endless treasures waited behind those doors. We would open the doors, pull the strings attached to the lightbulbs, and find ourselves lost for hours looking through boxes and trunks.

The basement was even better. There we found two massage beds with rollers that my grandfather used to relieve his arthritis. We would switch them on and let the rollers do their magic. A huge metal furnace that once provided heat to the house stood in the middle of the room with a trunk and arms like a huge oak tree. We discovered a few beds, a table and chairs, and a chest with drawers—all open game for exploration and imagination.

One of the coolest things about Grandmother's house was the narrow alley that ran behind it and behind all the houses on Freeman and McCreary Avenue all the way to Griffith. We walked this alley often and dreamed of the people who lived in houses we passed. Many of the houses were old, and we were convinced they were haunted.

I remember three-minute eggs at Grandmother Kittinger's house. She would boil the eggs and then put them in little, egg-shaped cups. She would gently break each egg on the top and remove the shell around that opening, and we would dig in with a spoon, adding a little salt and pepper. I remember eating grapefruit at Grandmother's house. She always used her colorful Fiesta dinnerware, and we would dig the grapefruit out with a spoon that had serrated edges on top.

At the farm where my mom's parents lived, I remember Granddad saying grace at dinner. Granddad was a faithful Catholic, and when he said grace, it was the same grace at every dinner. He said the prayer so fast that I never quite understood the words until I was older. I remember eating popcorn in his family room. He always held the bowl, and when we wanted to reach in and get handfuls, he would always say, "One piece at a time." I also remember Grandmother Grant making divinity candy.

After Grandmother Kittinger passed, we sold her home a few years later. My other grandparents' house is now occupied by my cousins. Home is a place where you mature, grow, and leave. It is a beautiful and melancholy mystery.

We recently built a new home in the midst of much change. Luke and Kellie have both graduated from college. Kellie is in the beginning of her career, and Luke is in law school. Additionally, Carrie's parents decided to sell their family home in New England and relocate to Oklahoma. They were ready to retire, and New England winters and taxes had taken their toll. Mom, now in her eighties, had decided she was ready to downsize. We all were leaving homes. Yes, home is a place you leave.

We have raised our kids, whose lives have mostly been lived in our previous home on West Dallas Street. It was a treasure trove of memories. Yet, we left the past to accommodate the growth of the future. We built a home with more space to accommodate our kids and their future families when they journey to be with us on future holidays and vacations. We are dreaming of grandkids, grandnieces, and grandnephews. We built a wing for Mom so she can continue to live independently but be close and have less house to care for. And we welcomed a new season with Carrie's parents as neighbors.

Carrie's parents left behind property that has been in the family for two generations. They both grew up in the town of North Reading, Massachusetts, though they spent their lives circling the globe in the United States Air Force. After a twenty-eight-year stint in the air force living all over the world and an additional twenty years in Massachusetts, they left home to make a new home in Oklahoma.

A Place You Return To

Though home is a place we leave, it is also a place where we return. Though my kids both live in town, their time under our roof ended all too soon for Carrie and me. We got a foretaste of this the summer of 2012, between Luke's junior and senior year of high school, when he joined the summer staff of Shepherd's Fold Ranch. Both kids had grown up going to the camp since their middle school years, so the Fold had played an important part in their spiritual formation. It was a place where they made many friends and mentors, where they had grown in their faith and encountered the Lord in a personal way. It is where they were baptized and where they baptized others in their commitments to Christ. Even though this was a volunteer position and Luke would receive no compensation, Carrie and I couldn't imagine a better place for him to spend the summer. What we didn't consider was the cost to our hearts of him being gone all summer.

We felt birth pangs from the change in our home; Luke was no longer there day in and day out. Throughout that summer, he came home for less than twenty-four hours a week, from Saturday afternoon to Sunday morning. He spent some of that time with us at home, resting. The remainder he spent with his friends, enjoying his only free time of the summer.

Throughout the fall, Carrie and I grew in anticipation as we helped Luke navigate the decisions of his future. He was excited to make the decision to attend the University of Oklahoma in Norman. He had a ball while running cross-country and especially while playing soccer that senior year, which we enjoyed as well. But he was "oh so done" with high school. His sights were not on the present or the past, but on the future. Carrie and I were excited about both of our kids' futures as well. Even so, Luke's rapid charge toward the future pained our hearts. We loved our family, and we loved our home. We knew that we couldn't cling to what used to be, yet it was hard to let go of what we had.

The following summer, Luke again worked at Shepherd's Fold. Same song, second verse. This time the cost was greater, as we knew when he returned home, he would be heading for college. He continued to work at the Fold each summer after his freshman and sophomore years, with Kellie joining him on staff in 2015, the summer she graduated from high school. In summer 2016, Luke took an internship in Norman. Kellie traveled a few times with friends and with Young Life that summer, as well as taking summer school classes and working. Suddenly our life had changed, and our home had changed.

I don't know why this caught Carrie and me off guard. Maybe we didn't anticipate it happening so soon. During my college years, I went home every summer and worked. Yet, once I graduated from college, I never lived at home again. However, I always returned home. I went home for most holidays, returning to be with my family. I didn't return for the house, but for the people. Wherever Mom and Dad were, that was home.

Sometimes all of us siblings were together. As we all got married and started families, wherever Mom and Dad lived was still our home base. This was the place to return to—the place of origin, of love, acceptance, wrestling, becoming, and faith. Even though we now had our own homes, this was also home. It was forever a part of our story.

Home is not static; nothing ever is. Home changes. Dad is now in heaven, along with Cindy, Dan, my grandparents, and all others who have gone before. The dynamics of home change. The people of home change (kids get married and add spouses, and there are new grandkids, new nieces and nephews) and the places of home change (new houses and new cities). Yet home remains.

Our Ultimate Journey

Ultimately, the vision of home guides my heart in this business of living and what matters most. All our journeys are going somewhere. Some of us are running from things we don't understand. Others are running toward things they hope for and desire. In the end, I believe we are all on a journey home. Home to the place of our beginning, where God spoke our name before time began. Home to the place of our belonging, to the eternal Father and his family, where we are fully known and fully loved. Home to the place of our becoming, where we received our place and calling in this world. Home to the place of our wrestling, where we dared to believe that the things God had in store for us were not too good to be true. Home to the place of our faith, where we finally see with our eyes all that we have held in our hearts.

This home is the ultimate home base and our heart's true home. It is like the North Star that we follow as we journey through life. It is not vague and undefined. Heaven is mentioned over six hundred times in Scripture, and Jesus talked about it on many occasions. This is where he came from and where he returned. He said he was going before us to prepare a place for us.

> *Do not let your hearts be troubled. You believe in God; believe also in me. My Father's house has many rooms; if that were not so, would I have told you that I am going there to prepare a place for you? And if I go and prepare a place for you, I will come back and take you to be with me that you also may be where I am. You know the way to the place where I am going."*
>
> *Thomas said to him, 'Lord, we don't know where you are going, so how can we know the way?' Jesus answered, 'I am the way and the truth and the life. No one comes to the Father except through me. If you really know me, you will know my Father as well. From now on, you do know him and have seen him.'* (John 14:1-7)

Jesus was going home. And he was going to prepare a place for us in his home, our ultimate home. He himself is the way home. As we journey with this vision of home, the miracle is that it is not just for some far-off time when we finally arrive on the shores of eternity. Just as the idea of home encompasses so much more than the houses in which we live, so the idea of heaven, our eternal home, encompasses so much more than our eternal destiny or final destination. In so many ways, heaven is for now!

Though the Father was in heaven, Jesus ushered in a new era and a new season on planet Earth—he brought the kingdom of heaven here. He declared, as John the Baptist did before him, *"The kingdom of heaven has come near"* (Matthew 3:2). He called his followers to live in the light of and to make our allegiance to this kingdom. Jesus described what this kingdom was like and demonstrated its values by the things he did. He told us of the riches, treasures, and joys of the final, full unveiling of this kingdom, and that we should direct our affairs now with those in mind.

He told us he would reveal to us the secrets of this kingdom (see Matthew 13:11) and give us the keys of the kingdom (see Matthew 16:19) to assist us with our journey. He also told many stories and parables to describe the kingdom. Stories recorded in the Gospel of Matthew that begin with, *"The kingdom of heaven is like"* . . .

treasure hidden in a field (13:44)

a mustard seed (13:31)

yeast worked through dough (13:33)

a net let down into the lake (13:47)

a landowner who went to hire workers for his vineyard (20:1)

a king who wanted to settle accounts with his servants (18:23)

a merchant looking for fine pearls (13:45)

a king who prepared a wedding banquet for his son (22:2)

New

Finally, just as we discard one house to move to another one, so God is doing the same in heaven. Scripture declares that there will be a new heaven and a new earth, and that the first heaven and earth will pass away (see Revelation 21:1). The next verse describes the new heaven as the new Jerusalem, the Holy City of God, *"prepared as a bride beautifully dressed for her husband"* (v. 2). Amazing! Don't we all love new things! We love new places and new clothes, new friends and new adventures, new cars and new homes. It is amazing that God is doing new things in the earth even today. The prophet Isaiah declared the words of God when he said, *"See, the former things have taken place, and new things I declare; before they spring into being I announce them to you"* (Isaiah 42:9). The apostle Paul described our new life in Christ as a new creation: *"The old has gone, the new is here!"* (2 Corinthians 5:17).

This is what God is up to—new things. In fact, in the revelation that John received on the island of Patmos, he heard God declare from his throne, *"I am making everything new!"* (Revelation 21:5). It evens says he will write on us his new name (see Revelation 3:12), and he will declare over us a new name (see Revelation 2:17).

We are living new lives, under a new covenant, filled with a new anointing of the new wine of his Spirit, while we are living under the authority of a new kingdom. All the while we are awaiting the new heaven and the new earth and his new name and our new names. We are living in a new era, and new things are coming.

CHAPTER 12

Simplicity Matters

My heart is not proud, Lord,
my eyes are not haughty;
I do not concern myself with great matters
or things too wonderful for me.

—Psalm 131:1

During my first year working as an auditor at Coopers and Lybrand, I was assigned to a variety of jobs and clients. I was the low man on the totem pole and would do whatever task was delegated to me by my senior auditor and audit manager. Auditing is about gaining assurance that the company you're auditing is not materially misstating representations made in their financial statements. It requires testing and examining records, systems, and procedures. Typically, as the job nears completion, a partner from the accounting firm will pay a visit to review his team's work. Since the partner is the one placing his signature on the report, he wants to ensure adequate work was done to justify his opinion about the client's representations.

I will never forget the first time a partner from Coopers and Lybrand visited one of my audits. He visited with me and my coworkers and encouraged us to do one thing: keep it simple. He used the acronym KISS and told us to "keep it simple, stupid." He also told us that he was like a bear in the woods, and he wanted our work to lead him through the woods; to leave a clear and simple trail to help him form the appropriate opinion.

Simplicity is easy to describe but harder to practice. The accounting partner I described loved the idea of simplicity, but for this young auditor attempting to satisfy his desire, I found the task nearly impossible. Maybe the gap of twenty-five years in our experience made a difference in our understanding of simplicity. I thought the path I cleared through the woods worked just fine. As I've grown older and added a few more years of experience under my belt, I've found that I see things with a little more clarity than I did in those younger years. Age and experience do that.

At my current job where I have worked for almost thirty years, one of my bosses constantly stresses simplicity. When working on a project, he is prone to say, "I want it so simple that a kindergarten student can understand it." I could respond by saying, "If you want the simplicity of a kindergarten student, you surely don't need a CPA with thirty-plus years of experience on the task." But I understand what he means. He is longing to simplify, to clarify, and to KISS.

Simplicity Beckons

I consider myself a pretty simple guy; straightforward, and a "what you see is what you get" type of guy. I think what drew me to the field of accounting in college were the simple concepts on which it is built: Assets = Liabilities + Equity; debits are on the left, credits are on the right. It gets much more complicated, but it is built on a simple and clear foundation. When things get overly complex, it's helpful to go back to the basics for the sake of clarity. When things are overly complex, they can stir distrust and unease. Maybe that is a weakness in me. Maybe it's true that all things are hard before they are simplified, I'm not sure. But I do know that simplicity beckons me.

I like simple music. Give me James Taylor and I am a happy man. If I'm going to play a board game, I like simple games with simple rules. If it takes thirty minutes to explain the rules, you've lost my interest. I like simple food, simple friends, and simple concepts. It isn't that I have anything against complexity or intricacy. I just have a love and appreciation for simplicity. To me, even the very word is inviting.

Simplicity is uncluttered, humble, and approachable. *Simple* means being unadorned, even plain, versus being elaborate and ornate. Simple is having nothing artificial. It is not luxurious, complicated, or complex, but basic and fundamental.

Simplicity is an idea that keeps me sane and grounded. As stated in the second law of thermodynamics and observed in the world around us, things don't evolve to order, but to disorder. Therefore, the longer we live, the more chaos and disorder we encounter. Simplicity helps bring order and structure to the disorder and chaos. As we grow in maturity and responsibility, the complexity of life increases, which is both natural and proper. Simplicity helps me navigate this complexity.

Simplicity of Design

I cannot be all things to all people. If I try to please all the people all the time, I will fail. The best thing I can do is to be authentically me. The great challenge in this is that many of us don't like who we are and what we see in the mirror. It is interesting that we are always comparing ourselves with others, trying to measure ourselves by unbelievably high standards. We hold others to lower standards and offer them grace if they fall short, but we never let ourselves off the hook.

A flamingo can only be a flamingo, as a bear can only be a bear. If a hummingbird attempts to soar like an eagle, he will fail miserably, and vice versa. Who can imagine an eagle attempting to flutter her wings and suck nectar out of the blooming flowers?

All of creation was made for a particular purpose, some numerous and varied, and some very specific. Whatever the purpose, that is the highest and best use of each creation. Only God the creator knows the purpose and meaning in all of creation, and discovering that purpose is our destiny.

When we create, we follow suit; like our creator, we create things for a purpose. We created hammers for the purpose of driving nails, and screwdrivers for driving screws into things. Man created torches for heat, ovens for cooking, calculators for help with mathematics, and radios and television for broadcasting. Purposes should not get crossed—a radio will not help me prepare dinner, and an oven will not help me with my math problem. I could possibly attempt to use a screwdriver to drive a nail, but how much more effective to use a hammer!

Whoever you are and whatever God has whispered in your heart to be, be that. Take all the pressure off to attempt to be what others would like you to be, and instead be fully you.

I love that Jesus, in such a simple and straightforward way, summarized what God had been communicating to man throughout all of history. It is not that he didn't have any more to say, because he said a lot. He spoke about many things and talked profoundly on many topics. However, when someone asked him what the greatest commandment was, his response was simple and straightforward.

> *One of the teachers of the law came and heard them debating. Noticing that Jesus had given them a good answer, he asked him, 'Of all the commandments, which is the most important?'*
>
> *'The most important one,' answered Jesus, 'is this: "Hear, O Israel: The Lord our God, the Lord is one. Love the Lord your God with all your heart and with all your soul and with all your mind and with all your strength." The second is this: "Love your neighbor as yourself." There is no commandment greater than these.' (Mark 12:28-31)*

We have a tendency to complicate and clutter, to confuse and pile on, layer after layer. It appears that this has been mankind's tendency throughout history. When God spoke to Moses on Mount Sinai, he gave him ten simple commandments to deliver to his people. Through the generations,

God's people added layer upon layer until there were hundreds of laws, regulations, and traditions in the faith.

The Gospel of Mark records a time when some Pharisees and scribes, who were folks that loved to talk about laws, inquired of Jesus about why he and his followers didn't observe all of their traditions. The issue they chose to address was crucial to spiritual health: handwashing! Really? Jesus cut to the crux of the matter.

> *"He answered them, 'Isaiah prophesied correctly about you hypocrites, as it is written: These people honor Me with their lips, but their heart is far from Me. They worship Me in vain, teaching as doctrines the commands of men. Disregarding the command of God, you keep the tradition of men.' He also said to them, 'You completely invalidate God's command in order to maintain your tradition!'"* (Mark 7:6-9 HCSB).

It is not just our faith we complicate. We do this to just about everything we touch. For example, when President Woodrow Wilson signed into law what is now the Internal Revenue Code in 1913, it was approximately twenty-seven pages in length. By 2016, it had ballooned to over seventy-four thousand pages in complexity. Man complicates, Jesus simplifies. He takes something as important as our faith in God and summarizes it in such a clear and concise way that no one can forget it: Love God. Love others.

Simplicity of Life

I encourage you to simplify. Simplicity brings clarity. It allows you to declutter and to focus. It helps you to keep the main thing the main thing; to focus on the major things and leave the minor things alone. It isn't that minor things have no value, it's just that they pale in comparison to the major ones. Minor things can pile up and become a mountain that obscures the view of what is really important. When you're distracted by minor things, it's hard to focus on what matters most. Distraction truly does lead to destruction.

I have a friend who likes to say he is a one-string banjo. He is a humble, Southern gentleman, and, in his self-deprecating way, he is basically saying that "what you see is what you get." I disagree with his self-assessment, as I have found him to be a profoundly talented individual. Yet, maybe the reason I see his talents and gifts so clearly is that he has chosen to be the best one-string banjo he can possibly be.

Simplification is easier said than done. Recently I have gone through one of the busiest seasons of my life, and simplification has seemed more of a good idea than a reality. I have had more things going on at one time than I thought humanly possible. As an example, over the course of a week in 2017, my sister left us for her heavenly home, Luke graduated from college, and Kellie left us for a month-long mission trip to Myanmar. Every situation was complex. Cindy's care team fell apart the last few weeks of her life, resulting in changing hospice organizations on her very last day. Luke was finishing his senior project and studying for finals, while driving back and forth to Tulsa to be with our family. Kellie got a terrible ear infection during the week before her departure. Needless to say, we were all emotionally, physically, mentally, and spiritually spent.

In the complexity of such moments, when simplicity isn't readily available, I find myself asking, "What is the most important thing I can do today?" In the crush and the insanity of all the noise, rush, and activity, this simplifying question brings clarity. I can even apply it to the moment, not just to the day. What is the most important thing I can do at this very moment? Always return to simplicity. Simplify your life, and simplify your thoughts. In the difficulty of complex times, you can take steps to simplify. Take a deep breath, then ask yourself what the most important thing is that you can do right now, this day, this moment.

Simplicity Is Costly

As with all things of value, simplicity comes at a cost. To narrow your focus to what is most important means that lesser things get deferred, ignored, or forgotten altogether. Simplicity helps to answer the call of what matters most. If, for example, I desire to clean my garage so I can use it for what it was designed—the parking and protection of my cars—then I need to make some decisions about everything else that has come to find its home there. The same is true for the clothes in my closet. My closet can only hold so much stuff. Therefore, if I continue to get new clothes, I must make some decisions about what stays and what goes.

I had an aunt who was a borderline hoarder. We visited her Florida home periodically through the years. Later in her life, we noticed that things began to accumulate. She had piles of newspapers, magazines, and clippings that she determined were important to keep. Though her kitchen shelves were filled with china, throughout her family room and dining room were boxes containing alternative sets of tableware and china. I guess she felt like one could never have too much china. The truth was, she was unwilling to pay the price to simplify. The result was a significant clutter, unbecoming of her home and life.

Simplification requires aggressive reinforcement. To keep yourself unburdened, you must be vigilant and alert to the clutter, the piles, and the complexity that continuously climb their way into your garage, closet, and home. As you consider the most important thing you can do at a particular moment, other things will shout, vying for attention. Only you can determine if there is room.

Who Says You Can't Have It All?

An old advertisement coined the phrase "Who says you can't have it all?" Well, I hate to be the bearer of bad news, but it isn't true. In trying to gain the world, you really can lose your soul. And in trying to grab all you can, you can lose what matters most.

I have few regrets about the life I've lived. I have had a great job. Early on, I made value decisions about what kind of job I wanted and what I wasn't willing to sacrifice for work. Due to important matters at my work, I have made sacrifices and missed some family functions. I remember when, early in my years with the company I work for, TCIX Rail, I had purchased tickets for Carrie and me to celebrate our anniversary with dear friends by going to see Broadway's traveling version of Les Misérables, our favorite musical. As the date approached, my bosses informed me that I needed to be in Houston for an inspection of an ocean vessel that was delivering product to the states. The date of the landing was the exact date of the show. Carrie and I were terribly disappointed. Nevertheless, sacrifices are made for important things.

In the larger arc of my work life, I've been able to be at all important family functions and at almost every important event in the lives of my wife and kids. I have been an active part of my community, both at home in my neighborhood and in the church communities in which I have worshipped. I have volunteered countless hours in those church communities because I believe in the local church, its influence in the lives of its members, and its importance to the larger community around it.

I have been available to my extended family. I was available to help my mom during my dad's journey with Parkinson's disease and dementia. I was available to assist my sister and her family as they walked two members through the diagnosis of ALS. I have been able to give myself to friendship and discipleship. All of these were important to me. And because of their importance and my choices, other things suffered.

I haven't climbed corporate ladders or built a business empire. I haven't become an investment guru, studying the markets and understanding its moods and movements. I haven't become a topflight athlete, pushing myself to peak performance. I haven't become a good golfer. I haven't become an excellent musician. I haven't even pursued my hobby of scuba diving or flown to Miami to watch my beloved Dolphins play in their home stadium. If time and money were no object, I would do all these things. You truly can't have it all, so you choose.

What I chose was faithfulness to my work, and I've worked as unto God, doing my best while balancing life's priorities, serving the gentlemen I work for and those I work with. I have entrusted my savings to faithful people who study the markets and do their best to steward resources. I have pursued health, with regular exercise and daily nutrition. I play golf once in a blue moon.

I still pursue my love of music, listening regularly and even learning some of my favorite songs on the guitar. I had a chance to go scuba diving with friends a few years ago and had a ball, but I don't dive regularly. And finally, I've seen the Dolphins play twice in the past few decades with Luke, and I look forward to seeing them again.

We all choose what is important to us, and we reap the consequences of those choices. As I look back, I have few regrets. I'm thankful for the life that I have, the good relationships with my family and friends. I'm thankful I've had the courage to make choices that line up with the values of my heart. When I look back at those choices, my heart doesn't condemn me. Not that I've lived perfectly, no one can do that. Yet, I have done the best I could do with what I've been given and have lived what I believe to be true.

CHAPTER 13

Truth Matters

It is better to live naked in truth than clothed in fantasy.
—Brennan Manning

I love the ocean. I've always felt its magnetism and call. I love its vastness, majesty, and beauty. I love the shades of green and blue and the taste of the fresh, salty air. I love its waves and the adventure found on and beneath them. Since man's earliest days, the oceans have lured and beckoned us to come and to cross, to adventure and to explore. Yet, for all its beauty and majesty, the ocean is a dangerous and foreboding place. The same ocean whose winds and waves can propel us to soul-stirring adventure can also ravage us in soul-crushing devastation. Even then, the call of the ocean remains and should not be ignored. In answering, we should approach its majesty and wonder with the utmost reverence and respect.

Like the ocean, life is filled with majesty and beauty, wonder and awe, which call us to come and to cross, to adventure and to explore. We must answer this call. At the same time, we must recognize the danger and the tempest, the wind and the waves, and realize that for all the beauty and majesty, a fury is present that we must not ignore. As we answer life's call, we should approach it with the utmost reverence and respect.

It is my sincere belief that most people believe in ultimate truth; that right and wrong, good and evil exist and are knowable. In America's early life, our founding fathers penned the following words to the Declaration of Independence: "We hold these truths to be self-evident, that all men are created equal, that they are endowed by their Creator with certain unalienable rights, that among these are life, liberty, and the pursuit of happiness." This idea of self-evident truth was stated by the apostle Paul in his letter to the Romans, as follows: *"Since what may be known about God is plain to them, because God has made it plain to them. For since the creation of the world God's invisible qualities—his eternal power and divine nature—have been clearly seen, being understood from what has been made, so that people are without excuse"* (Romans 1:19-20).

I agree with these writers that truth is self-evident, both implanted in our hearts like a moral compass and embedded in the world around us. A sailor choosing to ignore a compass will get lost at sea or, worse yet, suffer devastating shipwreck. Likewise, ignoring truth revealed both in your heart and displayed in the world around you will result in loss. As we approach our lives with the necessary reverence and respect, we must look for truth. It is our compass and north star for navigating the beautiful and treacherous journey required of us.

Truth isn't meant to prohibit and constrain; it is meant to free. Jesus said as much: *"Then you will know the truth, and the truth will set you free"* (John 8:32). Many view God as a cosmic killjoy who has set us up for failure with his list of do's and don'ts. The do's seem onerous and heavy, and the don'ts seem inviting and desirable. From the apple in Eden to the tablets of Sinai and beyond, we have been pushing the boundaries and breaking the rules. We have been saying to God and to anyone else who may listen, "Don't tell me what to do, and don't try to fence me in." Our culture endorses this unconstrained freedom to be or do almost anything. The only offense is when someone shares a different opinion. When confronted with truth, many respond as Pilate did to Jesus, "What is truth?" inferring that truth is either unknowable, or even worse, nonexistent.

My family started attending church in my preteen years. Growing up in church helped me immensely and launched me in the lifelong pursuit of God I currently enjoy. Along the way, I unintentionally picked up a misconceived view of God that was more weighted toward justice and holiness than it was toward mercy and love. While it is true that God is holy and just, it's his kindness and love that lead us to relationship with him.

After graduating from college, I heard my pastor at the time preach a sermon that was a turning point in my understanding of God. The sermon was on the goodness of God and his heart toward his children. Interestingly, to illustrate this goodness and love, he preached on the Ten Commandments. Instead of the commandments being a list of do's and don'ts that regulate our behavior—behavior that is rewarded or condemned based on our performance—my pastor reframed them. The heart of the matter was that our heavenly Father wasn't demanding rigid compliance but was instead offering love and counsel. Since he knows the ultimate end of our decisions, either the blessings that come from following his counsel or the devastating loss that comes from ignoring it, he was offering his highest love and best advice.

As an example, he didn't say, "Thou shalt not commit adultery" to keep us from having pleasurable sex with anyone we wanted. He said it because he knew that our lives will be happier and healthier if we keep our sexuality within the boundaries of marriage. He didn't say, "Thou shalt not steal" because he wanted to limit our supply, but to enhance it. He knew stealing would harm us in every way. He told us that we should have no other gods before him, since he is the one and only true God. All other gods are false and misleading and are dead-end streets. He told us to honor our father and mother, not because they may or may not deserve it, but because we would be the better for it.

The reframing of these commandments was one of the most helpful things a pastor did for me in my early adult life. If I think that the Ten Commandments or any other of God's laws or precepts exist to regulate my behavior and performance, I eventually will fail and feel alienated from God. A life-altering change of perspective is to understand that God loves me so much that he gave me his highest and best advice, and shared with me his deepest thoughts and secrets on successful and fruitful living.

And he did this, not for the purpose of keeping me in line or to rebuke or judge me and to keep me from pleasure, but to bless me and encourage me and usher me into the best life possible. Our heavenly Father truly does know best.

Source of Truth

And that leads us to a really good question. What is your source of truth and the core beliefs that you hold most dear? Surely they come from somewhere. For many of us, almost all our most-cherished beliefs are handed down to us from our families. As we mature, we realize that among these beliefs are some we continue to cling to throughout our lives. These beliefs have stood the test of time and have been proven in the crucible of our lives. We trust them and stand on the solid foundation they provide. The apostle Paul said as much when, in writing to Timothy, he said, *"I am reminded of your sincere faith, which first lived in your grand-mother Lois and in your mother Eunice and, I am persuaded, now lives in you also"* (2 Timothy 1:5).

We find other things we choose to discard, as we discover them to be less helpful in living productive lives. The test of time and the trials of life help us in our discernment and understanding of what is true. These ideas may be hard to discard because they have belonged in our family for generations. However, as with all things false, we should release them for what is true and what is better.

So we receive from our families both of these things: we receive tested and proven foundation-building truths that we embrace and in turn deem worthy to pass on, and we also receive things that fall short and are unworthy of our embrace. I've heard these referred to as gener-ational blessings and curses. Our journeys are filled with both. Our role is to choose which to embrace. This is easier said than done and requires discernment to understand which are the blessings and which are the curses. We may think that by their very nature blessings are easy to distin-guish from curses. However, because they have been passed down from generations and have family strings attached to them, this discernment is more difficult than imagined.

Others

Though our families are the earliest soil where our core beliefs are nurtured and grown, other voices come into our lives and assist in the pruning and cultivation of those beliefs. These voices come from all walks of life and include pastors and teachers, neighbors and friends, and even screenwriters and authors. Life is filled with information that comes at us from a thousand different sources. As we sit in classrooms and in pews, and as we listen to lectures and sermons, we are exposed to many thoughts and ideas. The same holds true as we read books, watch movies, and listen to music. The world is filled with innumerable thoughts, good and bad. We choose which ones we embrace.

In our pursuit of truth, it helps us to understand our humanity and, therefore, our tendency to err and to sin. Because of this, we should approach our lives with humility. This is especially true in our search for truth and in our understanding of right and wrong. Just as we need discernment in handling generational blessings and curses, so we need discernment in choosing which voices we will embrace from the vast ocean of ideas along the pathways of our lives. Which voices can we trust? Among all the voices, there remain good and trusted ones. These, much like the voices of our families, are proven over time. Truth becomes evident and stands the test of time amidst the onslaught of competing and lesser ideas. It is purified in the furnace of life, where the dross burns and the gold remains.

Though truth remains does not mean it is without assault. New and competing ideas will always arise, begging to be noticed, demanding a place at the table with truth. People will argue and debate, testing the strength of the prevailing ideas. These lesser ideas won't yield peacefully. This competition of ideas is mentioned in the book of Proverbs. It states that both wisdom and folly are calling out to those who will listen, both selling their respective ideas. Only one is speaking truth. We choose which we embrace, and that decision is of utmost importance with tremendous implications for our lives.

Sir Isaac Newton gave credit to those who had gone before him when he said, "If I have seen further, it is by standing on the shoulders of giants." My dad was one of those giants for me. There was nothing false about Dad. There was no pretense and certainly nothing fake or phony. He was who he was, and he didn't try to make you think he was more than that. Knowing Dad, he would probably be irritated that I'm writing about him because he never wanted attention on himself. He would turn the conversation to you or to his relationship with Jesus, the things he believed had much more value. It wasn't that he had low self-esteem, he just had his esteem in the right place.

As far as integrity, I've never met a person with more. I have heard integrity defined as wholeness; being undivided or unbroken. In layman's terms, it means that what you see is what you get and that you practice what you preach. I'm unsure if he internally felt the wholeness that those of us who knew him witnessed, but we can attest that it was there in his life in great measure. Though his words were few, they were as good as gold. If he gave you his word, you could count on it. You always knew who Don Kittinger was and who he was going to be. He was a man of character and integrity, and he was always going to remain just that. You could count on it.

He was a strong but simple man. His positions were clear. He was loving and tender but firm in his beliefs. He didn't offer advice freely but was always available to his family, friends, and anyone who needed him. He didn't live for the praise or accolades of others but did what he believed to be the right thing to do. He didn't do it for money, fame, or position but because it was right.

Dad loved because love is to be shared. His love wasn't overly verbal to us kids or to his friends (though it was to my mom), but it was more powerful than words. He demonstrated it in his actions each and every day. He was present with us and aware of us as he led and cared for our family. I am grateful to stand on Dad's shoulders.

My mom equally contributed to my footing and the foundation on which my life is built. There is not a day when I can say I ever felt unloved. I know that Mom is always in my corner, believing in me and cheering for me. No matter where I've gone or what I have done, I have felt her love, pride, and support. And all the while, she has held on to me loosely, letting me fly and go where God directs, trusting that all will be well. She is a never-ending voice of support and encouragement. She has also been an example of hospitality and a constant reminder of the importance of offering kindness to those we meet.

And there are others. Grandparents and youth leaders, choir directors and teachers. There are also dear friends. So as we navigate life, we pick up these ideas handed down to us from those on whose shoulders we stand. We discern truth and embrace it. From Dad I was handed humility and integrity, and from Mom love and kindness. From Richard Black, my dear friend and mentor, I was handed vision to pursue my dreams. From his wife, Linda, who cared for me like a mom, I was handed an infectious enthusiasm and love for others. From Carolyn Webb, my friend's mom and my high school youth leader, I was handed an unbridled passion and love for Jesus. From Ray Gregg and Terry Unruh, my favorite professors at Oral Roberts University, I was handed a belief in myself; that I was smart and able to accomplish anything.

The Big Idea of Truth

As we proceed through life, we come to understand many things. We learn the law of gravity by jumping off things. Even if we're poor at math, we learn that two plus two equals four. We learn that there are sixty seconds in a minute, sixty minutes in an hour, and twenty-four hours in a day. We learn that there are seven days in a week, and there are 365 days in a year. We learn from experience and observation, and we also learn from textbooks and encyclopedias.

In our day, information has never been more available and accessible. We have a rapidly expanding knowledge base. Engineer Buckminster Fuller created what he termed the "Knowledge Doubling Curve" back in the 1980s. An industrytap.com article states his findings: "He noticed that until 1900 human knowledge doubled approximately every century. By the end of World War II knowledge was doubling every 25 years. Today things are not as simple as different types of knowledge have different rates of growth. For example, nanotechnology knowledge is doubling every two years and clinical knowledge every 18 months. But on average human knowledge is doubling every 13 months. According to IBM, the build out of the "internet of things" will lead to the doubling of knowledge every 12 hours" (http://www.industrytap.com/knowledge-doubling-every-12-months-soon-to-be-every-12-hours/3950).

I find Mr. Fuller's premises easy to believe, considering the advancements I've witnessed in my lifetime. And though I consider myself a reader and a learner, the longer I live, the more I realize how little I know about a multitude of things. Instead of feeling more confident in the breadth of my knowledge, the more humble I grow from understanding how little I know. Another writer expressed this sentiment when he wrote this: "Because of our accelerating rate of learning, a few writers declared we must be in the age of 'the end of science.' This stance is hard to maintain for more than a nanosecond in view of the current state-of-belief in physics: that 96% of all matter and energy in our universe is some unknown variety we call dark. It is clear that 'dark' is a euphemism for ignorance. We really have no idea what the bulk of the universe is made of. We find a similar state of ignorance if we probe deeply into the cell, the brain, or even the earth. We don't know nothin'" (https://kk.org/thetechnium/the-expansion-o/). My sentiments exactly.

The writer goes on to say these words: "Thus even though our knowledge is expanding exponentially, our questions are expanding exponentially faster. . . . We have no reason to expect this to reverse in the future. The more disruptive a technology and tool is, the more disruptive the questions it will breed. We can expect future technologies such as artificial intelligence, controlled fusion, and quantum computing... to unleash a barrage of thousands of new huge questions—questions we could have never even thought to ask before. In fact, it's a safe bet that we have not asked our biggest questions yet. Or to put it another way, we have not yet reached our maximum ignorance" (https://kk.org/thetechnium/the-expansion-o/). The more we know, the more we realize how much we don't know. And the more we uncover and learn, the more we realize how much more there is to learn. Still, none of this should discourage us from setting our hearts on seeking truth and knowledge. We should, however, be humbled in our pursuit by the immensity of the task and by the discernment required for the journey.

If we're not careful, knowledge fatigue can take over and we can be overwhelmed by the immense and rapidly expanding world before us. However, in humility and simplicity, we can and should continue to sail and explore the vast ocean of knowledge and embrace truth. Truth becomes both our compass and our anchor, providing direction for our course and stability in the midst of the vast oceans on which we sail.

Make Every Effort

Over and over Scripture emphasizes remembrance, with a particular importance on writing things down so we don't forget them. God gave Jews in the ancient world instructions and encouragement to tie words as symbolic reminders on their hands and foreheads, clothing, and doorposts for the express purpose of keeping them foremost in their minds and hearts. That was because God knows that we are prone to wander and prone to forget.

I appreciate the passage in the first chapter of 2 Peter where three times Peter uses the expression "make every effort." When someone repeats words twice, they do so for emphasis, reflecting the importance of their words. When someone repeats words three times, they can't place any stronger emphasis on them. Here is the passage:

*For this very reason, **make every effort** to supplement your faith with goodness, goodness with knowledge, knowledge with self-control, self-control with endurance, endurance with godliness, godliness with brotherly affection, and brotherly affection with love. For if these qualities are yours and are increasing, they will keep you from being useless or unfruitful in the knowledge of our Lord Jesus Christ. The person who lacks these things is blind and shortsighted and has forgotten the cleansing from his past sins. Therefore, brothers, **make every effort** to confirm your calling and election, because if you do these things you will never stumble. For in this way, entry into the eternal kingdom of our Lord and Savior Jesus Christ will be richly supplied to you.*

*Therefore I will always remind you about these things, even though you know them and are established in the truth you have. I consider it right, as long as I am in this bodily tent, to wake you up with a reminder, knowing that I will soon lay aside my tent, as our Lord Jesus Christ has also shown me. And I will also **make every effort** that you may be able to recall these things at any time after my departure.* (2 Peter 1:5-15 HCSB)

Peter goes so far in verses 12 through 15 to discuss the importance of repetition and reminder. As a parent, my kids never liked for me to repeat the same thing over and over again. However, Carrie and I believed certain things were important enough to remind the kids time and again. They were valuable and worth repeating. Therefore, I can appreciate Peter's insistence that even though his readers already know these things, he will "always remind them about these things."

Paying Attention

Likewise, throughout Scripture there is an admonition to pay attention. I believe this is so important on our journey for truth. This is our one-and-only life, our one shot. We must pay close and careful attention so we don't miss the truth before us. Whether intentionally or not, we can ignore it, or we can merely overlook it. Paying attention is one of the most important things we can do. We can look, and we can listen. And, as noted earlier, we can "make every effort." What we give our attention to makes all the difference.

I encourage you to be a learner and to remain humble in this search for truth. I encourage you to remind yourself to pay attention to the things that are most important. Think about them, meditate on them, write them down, and put them in prominent places in your home and in your office, in your journal, and on your desk.

To what are you paying attention? What are you thinking about? Whatever it is, this choice determines your destiny and success. I encourage you to look to God as the source of truth. He is the creator and sustainer of everything. He knows all mysteries and secrets and discloses them as we pursue knowledge. Some choose to see God as narrow and confining. I believe the exact opposite is true. Our heavenly Father, like the universe he created, is expansive and endless. I believe the more we explore him, the more we will realize how much more there is to discover and how little we really know. As Paul prayed for us, *"may we be able to comprehend the length and width, height and depth of God's love"* (Ephesians 3:18 HCSB), even though here on earth we will never attain all there is to know about him and his boundless truth.

CHAPTER 14

Honor Matters

She's got a way about her.

—Billy Joel, "She's Got A Way"

We all have ways about us. The way we walk. The way we speak. The little routines we perform each day, the little tics and traits that identify us. I recently watched a video recording of myself and realized that in many ways I sounded like my brother, Greg. Sometimes I notice mannerisms in my kids and see glimpses of myself there also. We shouldn't be surprised that family members share ways. Ways rub off. They are contagious.

This is why our parents have told us forever that who our friends are is so important. I remember when, during Luke's junior high years, he made a new friend. As they spent time together, his ways rubbed off on Luke. I noticed that Luke picked up some of his mannerisms, even dressing and sounding like him.

The Wake of Life

The way we speak or dress are small things compared to the weightier issues of life. Just as our family and friends influence our ways in these lesser issues, so they also influence our ways in the larger issues. Dr. Henry Cloud writes about this influence in his book *Integrity: The Courage to Meet the Demands of Reality*. He compares our influence on each other to the wake that a boat leaves behind as it motors through the water. Dr. Cloud writes as follows:

> "The wake is the results we leave behind. And the wake
> doesn't lie and it doesn't care about excuses. It is what it is.
> No matter what we try to do to explain why,
> or to justify what the wake is, it still remains.
> It is what we leave behind and is our record."

You are leaving a wake. What do you want that wake to be?

"Little Christs"

Some don't like the label "Christian" and offer excuses about why. Some point back to the period of the Crusades and the evil done in the name of Christ. Some don't like organized religion, period. Others prefer an alternative label such as "disciple" or "follower of Jesus."

I like the label. Scripture states that *"the disciples were first called Christians at Antioch"* (Acts 11:26). I have heard it explained that followers of Jesus were identified with his name because they so reminded people of Jesus. They were "little Christs," people who were of the same character and nature as Jesus. I love this passage in Acts describing Peter and John:

> *"When they saw the courage of Peter and John and
> realized that they were unschooled, ordinary men,
> they were astonished and they took note that
> these men had been with Jesus"* (Acts 4:13).

Peter and John were two of Jesus' closest friends. Whenever Jesus narrowed his company to a few, Peter and John were always there. They weren't perfect, mind you. John was preoccupied with position and power along with his brother James while Jesus was preparing for his crucifixion. And Peter, well, he flat out denied he knew Jesus when it mattered the most. He betrayed his best friend. Despite their imperfections, Peter and John stayed near Jesus. When they messed up, they didn't give up. And the presence of Jesus rubbed off on them and transformed them—so much so that when people encountered them, they recognized that they had been with Jesus.

Jesus left a wake of influence that is still transforming lives today. Others have lived courageous lives with significance and purpose and have left a tremendous wake. Many have touched us in profound ways. Some are significant figures in history. Others are ordinary men and women: moms and dads, pastors and teachers, coaches, mentors, and friends. Our lives matter, and what we do matters. We're always touching lives in one way or another.

Holy Ground

A few years ago, I was speaking with a friend who had recently visited the Holy Land. On the trip was an eighty-one-year-old priest who served as his group's spiritual guide each day. As they visited the sacred sites, the very places where Jesus walked and lived, the priest would approach the sites with reverence. Many in the group would kneel, some would pray, and some would kiss the ground on which they were kneeling. My friend conveyed that it wasn't long before he was compelled to join in their reverence. I understood, since Carrie and I had the privilege of visiting the Holy Land, and I can still feel the overwhelming reverence and awe elicited by our journey.

As our conversation evolved, we discussed the importance of honor. A current tendency and pull is to treat nothing as sacred or holy, whether faith, life, marriage, or family. Yet, Scripture has much to say about honor. It says we should honor God above all. It says we should honor our father and mother. It says that we should honor those in authority. It says we should honor our spouses, our families, our neighbors, and even our own bodies. It speaks generously of honor and bestowing honor, and encourages us to do the same.

In modern practice, we honor people only when we deem it appropriate, and that sparingly. Our tendency is to withhold rather than to bestow honor. In that we are unlike our heavenly Father. He is generous, we are stingy. And the condition appears to be getting worse. Dishonor is thrown around in abundance and no one is exempt—so much so that the question arises, is anything remaining worthy of honor? If our tendency to honor is diminished, surely we are diminished. If there is no honor, then we have lost touch with what is most valuable and sacred among us.

Simple Gestures

Honor is lived in simple and small gestures. Day by day, we can carry it out in little ways. It's always the little things that add up to the big things, and it is the little foxes that spoil the vine (see Song of Solomon 2:15). Honor is lived in the gracious way I speak to my wife and children. It's lived in how I treat my neighbors and coworkers. Am I generous with what I receive? Do I smile and greet people as our paths cross? Do I cheat on my taxes? The list goes on. If we don't honor in small things, giving honor where honor is due, neither will we honor in bigger things.

Choices Matter

Consequences follow every decision and choice we make. A segment of contemporary society is telling us to untether ourselves from the social constructs handed down to us; whether these constructs come from our nation, school, family, church, or religion, they should be questioned, challenged, and possibly discarded.

Nothing is wrong with critical thinking. However, if we choose to posture ourselves as skeptics and critics, we drift from honor. It's impossible to provide honor and dishonor simultaneously. When did we obtain such great insight to evaluate the world and to determine what is best? Throughout our lives, if we choose the path of understanding and desire to gain wisdom and discernment, we will grow step by step and day by day. This is an endeavor that takes great humility.

Honor and Humility

In the interim, as we wait, learn, and grow, we should do so with honor. Honor postures us with the humility appropriate to our position. We are part of the human race and the children of God. We weren't the first, and we won't be the last. Millions have come before us, and millions will follow. Our lives on this planet really are, as the Psalms declare, but a vapor and a wind. That is not a declaration that we are unimportant or insignificant. No, we are each precious and unique children of our God. Yet we are the children, and he is the father. We are the created, he is the creator. I love these verses in Hebrews that provides a proper perspective:

> *"For Jesus is considered worthy of more glory than Moses,*
> *just as the builder has more honor than the house.*
> *Now every house is built by someone, but the One*
> *who built everything is God"* (Hebrews 3:3-4 HCSB).

When we acknowledge that he is the father and we are the children, we give honor where it is due. When we acknowledge that creation belongs to him—the land, seas, and all that exists—we honor. When we walk in humility among our peers, in reverence to those who have gone before, and in thoughtful regard to those who will come after, we honor.

In contrast, pride exerts itself and insists on having its own way. It gives no thought to peers or forerunners or those who follow. It betrays history and gives full expression to its own thoughts and feelings regardless of consequences. It declares itself true and becomes its own standard and measure.

Choosing Honor

Some individuals abuse power and authority. They take advantage of their position and use it selfishly rather than for the common good. With their actions, they assault honor and all that it stands for.

Honor guards those under its watch and protection, and it fights for those less powerful. We have all seen or read of attacks on honor in ways both big and small. The list is endless and includes child abuse, assaults on women, racism, worker exploitation, bank fraud, and adultery, to name just a few. In recent generations, it has included such horrific actions as the Holocaust, the sexual abuse scandal in the Catholic Church, and now the rampant rise of the radical threat of jihad. The arc of the depravity of man in such deplorable and dishonorable actions can lead those in its wake to despair of life and to conclude there is no honor.

Honor is also assaulted in small ways. These may be more impactful because they touch our everyday lives. When we're overlooked and dismissed, we are dishonored. When our contribution is ignored or we're undervalued, we are dishonored. When our communication is interrupted or our ideas are dismissed, we are dishonored. Each such action begs us to conclude that there is no remaining honor. Is it possible to rise above such actions?

Yes!

The answer is yes! That doesn't mean it will be easy. As with anything good, it is never easy. Yet God created the world with honor and bestowed us with honor. He has instructed us in honor and, in Jesus, demonstrated how to live in honor. The choice is now ours: What will we choose?

Some like to muddy the waters by declaring that the choice isn't that simple. They pile on layer after layer of complexity and make the choice more difficult than it is. This helps justify their lack of accountability. If they can cast aspersions on truth and cloud every issue, then they can become a law unto themselves and do whatever they choose. In the world of their making, there is no black and white, only gray. But this is not the real world of the Father's making. And we are living in his world and under his rule and reign. He created the universe with his spoken word, including the fabric of morality, ethics, and conscience by which he desired us all to live.

Words

We live in a noisy world filled with words; words written, spoken, shouted, and sang. Words are important. Scripture teaches that God created with the power of his words and that we create that way too. It states that life and death are in the power of the tongue and that our words can both build up and destroy. We have felt the power of a timely word; the "I love you" that brings comfort and strength. We have also felt the blow of a word cutting us to the core.

Worthy and Worthless

Some words are more important than others; some worthy, others worthless. Pay attention to the worthy ones. I encourage you to listen to and to speak words that are life giving; words that strengthen and encourage, words that induce hope, words that embrace truth, and words that bestow honor. Even when words are corrective and for rebuke, these are also for our good. As the proverb states, *"Wounds from a friend can be trusted, but an enemy multiplies kisses"* (Proverbs 27:6).

GIGO

I have noticed in my life that everything I read, hear, and watch has an effect on me. The type of books, magazines, movies, and music that I embrace on any particular day can affect my attitude and disposition. Over months and years, their effect becomes ingrained in me. A wide spectrum of art exists, and my intention is not to criticize any particular genre or form. Still, I will venture to address a few.

I believe that pornography has no value and is destructive to the soul. I believe slasher movies have no value for society. I believe that if a person ingests a steady diet of violent and profane content, then that person can expect to become more violent and profane. A term used in the early days of computer programming is GIGO. This acronym stands for "garbage in, garbage out." I believe this is true of our lives. What we input through our choices of art, literature, and information will affect the tone and tenor of our lives.

This may be evident with certain content, such as slasher movies and porn. But it remains true of whatever we choose to ingest. I find that if I listen to a steady diet of rock and roll, my life takes a more frenetic pace. If I watch 24/7 cable news, I may be informed, but with the weight of all the bad news heavy on my heart. If the majority of my reading is money magazines, the majority of my thoughts will be about money. If I obsess with watching sports, sports become my obsession.

I am a music fan and enjoy rock and roll. I do watch the news and read the *Wall Street Journal* to keep informed. I do read money magazines to help steward my finances, and I am a sports fan and watch my fair share of sports. I could be consumed with these interests 24/7. In fact, I could choose any one of these and be entirely consumed, whether with music, news, money, or sports.

I have a sweet tooth with a particular fondness for dark chocolate. Even so, I know that chocolate should be an accessory to my diet, like a bow on a package, rather than the main course. Should I choose otherwise, I'll suffer the negative consequences. Likewise, if I choose to constantly ingest less honorable things, whether music, news, money, or sports, I will become the lesser for it.

Think of These Things

I want to remind you of the apostle Paul's words in his closing remarks to the church at Philippi:

"Finally, brothers and sisters, whatever is true, whatever is noble, whatever is right, whatever is pure, whatever is lovely, whatever is admirable—if anything is excellent or praiseworthy— think about such things" (Philippians 4:8).

I love this passage and the ideas it conveys; truth, nobility, excellence, and purity. Some things are better than other things; some are worthy of our consideration and thought, while others should be discarded. How do we navigate between the two? We know in our hearts. God has placed in the heart of man the knowledge of right and wrong, good and evil. I believe this is what Scripture means when it states that *"He has . . . set eternity in the human heart"* (Ecclesiastes 3:11).

In addition, we have thousands of years of history, giving us examples of those who have made both good and bad decisions. We see the patterns and the trail of evidence in their stories to help us navigate our own.

Furthermore, we have God's own story, his written Word. Through the years, I have become a reader, and words have become important to me, whether written, spoken, or put to music. One of my love languages is encouraging words. I'm sure my love for words has given me the courage to pen these pages for you.

His Words above My Words

I could write ten thousand words and they wouldn't carry the impact of one word uttered from the mouth of God. His words are filled with power and life. His words change the atmosphere and alter the course of history. His words transform and resurrect.

You may have a favorite author whose writing stirs your soul. I have a few of those. You might love the lyrics penned from a certain songwriter or poet. Personally, as I've said before, I'm a James Taylor and Bono fan. The truth is, the beauty and creativity found in such writing is a gift from the author of life. John's Gospel refers to this author as he begins writing:

"In the beginning was the Word, and the Word was with God, and the Word was God. He was with God in the beginning. Through him all things were made; without him nothing was made that has been made. In him was life, and that life was the light of all mankind. The light shines in the darkness, and the darkness has not overcome it" (John 1:1-5).

John is referencing the creation story found in the first pages of Genesis where God spoke things into existence and created through his proclamation. Scripture makes many powerful declarations about God and his word. It states that he elevates above all things his name and his word (see Psalm 138:2). It proclaims that although someday the heavens and the earth will pass away, replaced by a new heaven and a new earth, God's word is eternal and will never pass away. The prophet poetically penned, *"The grass withers, the flower fades, but the word of our God remains forever"* (Isaiah 40:8 HCSB).

God's written Word, the Bible, is an endless treasure trove of literature. It contains thousands of years of history. It houses poetry and romance, biography and lament. It contains books of wisdom and instruction, as well as writings from prophetically gifted individuals throughout history. Many of its words speak comfort, peace, and encouragement, while many others are challenging and difficult. Some people celebrate these words, while others despise them.

I have chosen to place the full weight of my hope and trust in them and in the God who stands behind them. When the words are difficult, and I stumble in my understanding, I declare with the apostle Peter, *"Lord, who will we go to? You have the words of eternal life"* (John 6:68 HCSB).

I have found them to be unlike any other words. I can read them over and over again, year after year, and they are never stale and never old. Like the prophet Jeremiah, I can declare, *"Your words were found, and I ate them. Your words became a delight to me and the joy of my heart"* (Jeremiah 15:6 HCSB).

I have also found that, as the writer of Hebrews declares, the *"word of God is living and effective and sharper than any double-edged sword, penetrating as far as the separation of soul and spirit, joints and marrow. It is able to judge the ideas and thoughts of the heart"* (Hebrews 4:12 HCSB).

So in your ways and in your words, in your actions, choices, and thoughts, I encourage you to honor. Honor in ways both small and large. Find the honor in the world around you, and let your contribution be one of honor. You will be following the examples of Jesus and many others who have gone before us living honorable lives. You will be the better for it!

CHAPTER 15

Jesus Matters

Of all the things I could write about or recommend to you for successful living and for living a life that matters, the best thing I could offer is a relationship with Jesus. Life is a miracle and filled with beauty. Yet, it is not easy, and there are many difficulties. We are birthed in struggle and pain, and the moment we're born, it's certain that one day we will also die. During our brief lives, we will encounter both joy and sorrow, pleasure and pain. How do we make sense of it all?

My parents were good people; the salt-of-the-earth type, hardworking and disciplined, loving and kind. They minded their own business and tended to their lives. Dad worked hard, excelling in his career as an air force pilot, and Mom was an amazing mother, loving and caring for us kids. They had great friends wherever they went and were always involved with others. My parents had been raised in church, but it wasn't personal to them, it was just religion. So, they abandoned attending church in their young adult years.

During these years, they searched for meaning and satisfaction in various places. When they witnessed the selfishness in my siblings and me in our early years, they decided to return to church in search for some moral grounding. What they found instead was an introduction to a relationship with Jesus. As they sat in church and heard the good news of the gospel of Jesus Christ, it was as if they heard it for the first time, this time embracing it and choosing to follow Jesus and receive him as their

Lord and Savior. It wasn't long before my brother, my sister, and I all met Jesus and received the love he offered.

Our relationships with Jesus transformed our lives and affected everything else that happened from that moment to this. The transformation has been both internal and external. The fruit of our relationship with Jesus has been seen and felt in qualities that have grown through the years in increasing measure. Qualities that include love, for ourselves and for others; joy, even in difficult and desperate circumstances; abiding peace; patience, not a natural gift for a Kittinger, at least for my mom and me; kindness; goodness; gentleness; faithfulness; and self-control. Scripture refers to these as the fruit of the Spirit; tangible manifestations of lives lived in relationship with Jesus.

I have witnessed such transformation both within my immediate family and within the larger family of God for over forty years now, and have borne witness to its fruit. Such fruit stands in contrast to the fruit of lives lived according to what Scripture refers to as the flesh or the spirit in the world. That fruit includes immorality and impurity, idolatry and hatred, jealousy, rage, and selfish ambition.

In reviewing these two ways of living—lives lived in relationship with Jesus and lives lived without—I'm sure you would agree that the choice seems like a no-brainer. Why would anyone choose the latter? Yet many do. Humanity wants to go its own way and do its own thing. We don't want to be told what to do. We don't want to yield to others, and we certainly don't want to be told we need a Savior to deliver us from ourselves. We can witness this independence even in toddlers, who love to say no. From the beginning of humanity, back in the garden, Adam and Eve rejected God's command and ate the forbidden fruit. We have always needed a Savior.

Jesus' best friends, Peter and John, both wrote that he was chosen as our Savior before the foundation of the world (see 1 Peter 1:20 and Revelation 13:8). What a mystery, that God would create humanity while knowing we would violate his trust and disobey his instruction and our salvation would require his ultimate sacrifice! All this so he could have a family.

If our existence ended with death and our time here was all there is, then our pleasure, happiness, and comfort would be all that mattered. While many may embrace this shallow philosophy at face value, in reality, for all of human history, mankind has believed in life after death. The apostle Paul describes this shallow thinking here:

For God's wrath is revealed from heaven against all godlessness and unrighteousness of people who by their unrighteousness suppress the truth, since what can be known about God is evident among them, because God has shown it to them. For His invisible attributes, that is, His eternal power and divine nature, have been clearly seen since the creation of the world, being understood through what He has made. As a result, people are without excuse. For though they knew God, they did not glorify Him as God or show gratitude. Instead, their thinking became nonsense, and their senseless minds were darkened. Claiming to be wise, they became fools and exchanged the glory of the immortal God for images resembling mortal man, birds, four-footed animals, and reptiles.

Therefore God delivered them over in the cravings of their hearts to sexual impurity, so that their bodies were degraded among themselves. They exchanged the truth of God for a lie, and worshiped and served something created instead of the Creator, who is praised forever. Amen. (Romans 1:18-25 HCSB)

We are without excuse and have from the beginning needed a Savior. Thanks be to God for providing one in Jesus.

One of my favorite songs from my early years as a Christian is "Jesus is the Answer" by Andraé Crouch. The chorus simply says this:

Jesus is the answer, for the world today,
Above Him there's no other
Jesus is the way.

It's a simple song with a simple message; God so loved the world, that he gave (see John 3:16). Despite God's generosity and the greatness of the gift, our nature is to fight it. We want to go at it on our own. We don't want to be needy. We don't want to be "saved" from anything, nor do we want to have a Savior. We want to work hard, and perform, and prove that we have what it takes. We want to believe in our inherent goodness and in our neighbor's. We want to earn our way in this life as well as in the next.

But this contradicts what the Bible says. The Bible says that all of us have sinned and fallen short of the glory of God (see Romans 3:23). The Bible says the human heart is *"more deceitful than all else and is desperately sick; who can understand it?"* (Jeremiah 17:9 NASB). The Bible says, *"There is no one righteous, not even one; there is no one who understands; there is no one who seeks God. All have turned away, they have together become worthless; there is no one who does good, not even one"* (Romans 3:10-12; see also Psalm 14:1-3; 53:1-3). The apostle Paul made the following confession in his letter to the Romans:

> *For I know that good itself does not dwell in me, that is, in my sinful nature. For I have the desire to do what is good, but I cannot carry it out. For I do not do the good I want to do, but the evil I do not want to do—this I keep on doing. Now if I do what I do not want to do, it is no longer I who do it, but it is sin living in me that does it.*
>
> *So I find this law at work: Although I want to do good, evil is right there with me. For in my inner being I delight in God's law; but I see another law at work in me, waging war against the law of my mind and making me a prisoner of the law of sin at work within me. What a wretched man I am! Who will rescue me from this body that is subject to death? Thanks be to God, who delivers me through Jesus Christ our Lord!* (Romans 7:18-25)

Recently, on a trip to Charlotte, North Carolina, I had the privilege of spending a few hours at the Billy Graham Library. It was a special time in a special place. Somewhere in the filmed presentations, Billy's son Franklin observed that what made his father so special was that he never spoke or wrote from his own perspective. He always began his speech or counsel with "the Bible says."

Billy clung to the Bible and embraced it as the very words and counsel of God. Somewhere else along my journey at the library, there was a recording of Billy recounting a time early in his ministry when some colleagues were debating the accuracy and inerrancy of Scripture. They were expressing doubt that the Scriptures were in fact God's words. Billy described leaving that discussion and going out into the night to pray. He laid his open Bible on a tree stump and conversed with God. Billy told God that there were many things he didn't understand, yet he chose to place his trust in God. He chose then and there that he would take God at his word and believe that the words contained in the Bible truly were the words of God.

From that moment on, Billy's life exploded. He shared God's Word and the salvation message of Jesus Christ on every continent and in countries too numerous to count. He influenced presidents and world leaders, politicians and movie stars, business executives and military generals. I was overwhelmed to learn that every US president from Truman to Trump requested an audience with him; thirteen consecutive presidents during Billy's adult lifetime. Many of these sought his counsel in their hours of greatest need; Eisenhower before sending troops into Little Rock, Johnson after the assassination of President Kennedy, Nixon during Vietnam, and George W. Bush after September 11. More importantly, he shared the simple gospel message with everyone he met. Some believe he shared the gospel with more people than any other person in history.

Hollywood sought to understand him. I saw interviews with Johnny Carson, Phil Donahue, and Woody Allen, all asking Billy why he believed what he believed. I saw pictures of him with world leaders, from Golda Meir to Mikhail Gorbachev, from the general secretary of China to the leaders of Eastern Europe, and various queens and kings from around the globe. What was it about him that drew all these people to meet him and hear what he had to say? The answer is Jesus.

Jesus was Billy's lifelong message. Billy shared that salvation is found in no other name, hope is found in no other name, peace is found in no other name, and life is found in no other name. The attention that Billy received is the result of the promise of Jesus, who said, *"And I, when I am lifted up from the earth, will draw all people to myself"* (John 12:32). Jesus is the central figure in history. He is the Messiah, the Savior, and the hope of the world.

Receive Him

So what do we do with Jesus? How do we now live, since we've been exposed to this truth that Jesus is the Son of God who died to reconcile us and to bring us into relationship with the Father of all.

First, you must receive him. How do you receive him? Just like you would receive any other gift: you open your hands and take it from the giver who freely offers it to you. And if you have manners, you thank the giver for their generosity. That's it.

Salvation is a free gift. It's available for all, even the very worst among us. The Bible tells us God desires no one to perish but all to receive salvation and come to a knowledge of the truth (see 2 Peter 3:9). For years Christians have used a few scripture verses found in Paul's letter to the Romans as a simple explanation of what it means to receive Jesus. They have coined these verses the "Romans Road" to salvation.

The Romans Road includes these verses:

1. *"For all have sinned and fall short of the glory of God"* (**Romans 3:23**).

   All have sinned. Everyone. We are all in need of a Savior. You talk about inclusivity! This includes the entire world.

2. *"For the wages of sin is death, but the gift of God is eternal life in Christ Jesus our Lord"* (**Romans 6:23**).

Here is both very bad news and unbelievably good news. The bad news is that since we are all sinners, if we stay in our sin, our destiny is death. The unbelievably good news is that God gave his Son to provide a different reality for all. This gift just needs to be received. The gift is eternal life, both now and for eternity.

3. *"But God demonstrates his own love for us in this: While we were still sinners, Christ died for us"* **(Romans 5:8).**

We didn't earn it. He loved us in our sin and still does.

4. *"If you declare with your mouth, 'Jesus is Lord,' and believe in your heart that God raised him from the dead, you will be saved"* **(Romans 10:9).**

Here is how you receive this gift: you acknowledge what he has done with your heart, soul, mind, and strength—that includes your mouth.

5. *"Everyone who calls on the name of the Lord will be saved"* **(Romans 10:13).**

When you accept his gift, you change your destiny.

6. *"Therefore, since we have been justified through faith, we have peace with God through our Lord Jesus Christ"* **(Romans 5:1).**

Peace comes through Jesus. The opposite is also true: no Jesus, no peace.

7. *"Therefore, there is now no condemnation for those who are in Christ Jesus"* **(Romans 8:1).**

8. *"For I am convinced that neither death nor life, neither angels nor demons, neither the present nor the future, nor any powers, neither height nor depth, nor anything else in all creation, will be able to separate us from the love of God that is in Christ Jesus our Lord"* **(Romans 8:38-39).**

These last two verses sound too good to be true. They describe our life in Christ once we have received him. We are no longer condemned due to our sins but are justified in Christ forever. We continue to confess our sins and lean into him as our justification from the day of salvation going forward, and we are never condemned. We will make mistakes, yet we are covered. We fall down, but he picks us up. We sin, and his grace covers our sins. And nothing will ever separate us from his love.

Confess Him

Once we have received Jesus and have confessed our sins to him and our need for a Savior, we continue to confess him for the rest of our days. This confession is like breathing. We exhale by confessing our sins, mistakes, and shortcomings, and we inhale by confessing Jesus as our Lord and Savior. Paul makes another powerful declaration in Romans when he states, *"I am not ashamed of the gospel, because it is the power of God that brings salvation to everyone who believes"* (Romans 1:16). We cling to Jesus and we trust in him and we surely are not ashamed of him. We should be ashamed of our sins but never of Jesus. Jesus said that if we confess him before others, he will confess us before his Father in heaven. He also said that if we disown him, he will in turn disown us before his Father in heaven (see Matthew 10:32-33).

Call upon Him

As we learned in the Romans Road, all who call upon the name of the Lord will be saved (see Romans 10:13). Calling upon God is not a one-time occurrence but should be our regular practice. Trusting him, we humble ourselves and call upon his name. Prayer is the vehicle through which we call upon him. Throughout Scripture, God encourages us to call upon him. So call upon him in good times and in bad. Call upon him from the lowest pit and from the highest mountain. God hears and answers prayer. Psalm 139 says there is nowhere we can go where God's presence is not there. Since God is everywhere, sees and knows all, and invites us to pour out our hearts to him, why would we hold back? Jeremiah 33:3

provides a strong reason to call upon him: he promises to show us great and awesome things.

Worship Him

Once you encounter Jesus, there truly is only one proper response, and that is worship. We see this response over and over again in Scripture: from the magi bringing their gifts; to the shepherds encountering the angelic choir; to the crowds on the banks of the Jordan River hearing John the Baptist declare Jesus as the Son of God; to the blind, sick, and lame responding to healing; to the individuals receiving revelation about everything they have ever done; to the lady caught in adultery accepting forgiveness of her sins. The response each time was worship. Even the mob who arrived in the garden of Gethsemane to arrest Jesus, when hearing him declare his identity, *"drew back and fell to the ground"* (John 18:6), an involuntary response of worship. The Roman soldier who witnessed the manner in which Jesus died, proclaimed, *"Surely he was the Son of God"* (Matthew 27:54), another declaration of worship.

Worship is the proper response for those who encounter the living God and his precious Son, Jesus. Paul, who encountered Jesus on the road to Damascus, was blinded and knocked to the ground by God's presence. Moses, when he encountered God in the burning bush on Mount Horeb, took off his shoes in response to the holiness of God. The prophet Isaiah, when encountering the revelation of God, declared that he was undone and thought that he would die.

The Bible says that at the end of time, every knee will bow and every tongue confess that Jesus is the Lord (see Philippians 2:10-11). Those of us who love him and have received him will proudly confess and offer our worship. At that time even those who reject him will bow the knee and confess his praise. It will be unavoidable, like the mob falling back or like the soldier declaring that this is the Son of God.

Develop a Relationship with Him

As we have opportunity today, let us pursue him. Yesterday is past, and the future is not yet here, so today is all we have. Let us pursue a relationship with Jesus in the now of our life. Let us make him our highest goal, our most treasured possession, and our dearest friend. You develop a relationship with Jesus just like you would with any other friend; you spend time with him and get to know him. If you're really going to be friends, you must be vulnerable and share your true self. Otherwise, the relationship will be shallow. He knows you intimately anyway, so why not take the risk and be vulnerable?

Jesus accepts you just as you are. You don't have to clean yourself up or wait until you're ready to make something of yourself. He wants to be your friend today. We exclude ourselves by thinking he doesn't want us as we are. We insist on being a better version of ourselves prior to coming to him. But Jesus wants a relationship with the real you. He doesn't want some idealized version that may arrive at some future date.

It's exhausting to try to be someone you're not. I'm so grateful that Jesus came for me as I am and not as I should be or could be or might be or will be. One of my favorite passages of Scripture is where Jesus invites us to come to him:

> *"Come to me, all you who are weary and burdened,*
> *and I will give you rest. Take my yoke upon you and learn*
> *from me, for I am gentle and humble in heart, and*
> *you will find rest for your souls. For my yoke is easy*
> *and my burden is light"* (Matthew 11:28-30).

Jesus was regularly criticized by religious people because of his choice of friends; cheats, adulterers, and sinners of all kinds. None of them had cleaned up their act prior to their friendship with Jesus, but that friendship revolutionized their lives. Jesus said that he came for sinners, like you and me. When religious leaders challenged his choice of friends, Jesus replied in this way:

"It is not the healthy who need a doctor, but the sick.
I have not come to call the righteous, but sinners" (Mark 2:17).

Jesus came for friendship with you. Don't refuse his invitation. It will revolutionize your life.

Honor Him

No person or idea is more worthy of honor than Jesus. It's clear throughout Scripture that God is a God of honor and that he chooses to reserve the highest honor for his beloved Son. The Bible declares, *"God exalted him to the highest place and gave him the name that is above every name"* (Philippians 2:9). No other name is like the name of Jesus!

This world casts much dishonor at Jesus. Many use his name as profanity. Additionally, I'm shocked at the scorn cast upon Jesus by religious people of various faiths. When I visited Israel in 2015, I traveled all over the tiny country. One of my favorite spots was the Western Wall at the Temple Mount. This is the very place proclaimed throughout Scripture as the mountain of God. Many believe it to be the place of Abraham's offering of his son Isaac to God, and possibly the same place, or very near it, where God sacrificed his only Son, Jesus. On this same mountain sits the Dome of the Rock, Islam's oldest historic building. I was troubled to learn that on this holy site, words inscribed in Arabic on the outside of the dome, in effect, said, "Allah is God, and he has no son."

Other religions claim that Jesus was a prophet or a good man yet deny his sovereignty. However, if Jesus isn't the Messiah as he claimed, then he can't be a good man but instead a liar. He is either the Messiah, or a deceiver and false prophet. He can't be both. Either he is who he said he was, or he isn't. Every person is now faced with the decision, What will you do with Jesus? Who do you believe he is? If you believe he is the Son of God, then honor is your proper response to him.

Love Him

Finally, as you grow in Jesus by pursuing the things described above—by receiving him, confessing him, calling upon him, worshipping him, by developing a relationship with him, and by honoring him—you can't help but fall in love with him. To know Jesus is to love him. I have been following Jesus since I met him as a boy. The more I learn of him, the more my heart grows in affection and the more I want to be near him.

I can get my fill of church, and I can reach my fill of sermons, songs, or books. And I love people, but I can reach the point where I need some space and room to breathe. Yet, I have never reached that point in my relationship with Jesus. The more I get to know him, the more I encounter his goodness. He is filled with love and affection, and he speaks blessing and hope. He has boundless compassion and never gives up on me. Get to know Jesus, and tell me if you don't feel the same. Of all the things that matter, Jesus matters most.

About the Author

Danny is the CFO of TCIX Rail based in Tulsa, Oklahoma, where he has served for almost thirty years. He and his wife, Carrie, are the founders and directors of Sons and Daughters International.

Danny graduated with a bachelor of science in accounting from Oral Roberts University and earned his CPA while working at Coopers and Lybrand. After short stints at Property Company of America and Impact Productions, he has built his career working at TCIX Rail.

Danny accepted Jesus as his Lord and Savior as a preteen and has spent his life pursuing and being pursued in a relationship with the mystery that is God: Father, Son, and Holy Spirit. His identity as God's beloved son is the most important thing about him. Danny is a thinker who loves to read, write, and journal, he has a passion for music, and is a family man and friend. Following Jesus has been the greatest adventure of his life. Danny has been married to his best friend for over thirty years, and they are the parents of two adult children, Luke and Kellie.

Danny has served in a variety of capacities, including serving his local church and various boards. He has led multiple spiritual retreats to encourage others in their walk with Christ, led marriage retreats, and taught various classes on faith, family, marriage, and parenting. Danny has been a featured speaker at men's gatherings and has led small groups for many years. However, his greatest joy is found in his own spiritual journey and being a friend to others.

In recent years, Danny has been sharing what he has learned, through conversations, coaching, speaking, and writing. If you would like to contact him, find out more information, purchase books, or request Danny to speak, please contact:

Danny Kittinger
danny@dannykittinger.com
dannykittinger.com

Sons and Daughters International

All proceeds from the sale of this book go to fulfill the mission of Sons and Daughters International.

Sons and Daughters International is a charitable 501(c)(3) organization dedicated to resourcing the kingdom of God in relational and practical ways. We offer gifts of leadership, vision, encouragement and teaching for the purpose of building, strengthening, and expanding the Body of Christ and for growing in relationship with God and each other.

To learn more, please contact us at:

Sons and Daughters International
P.O. Box 700383
Tulsa, OK 74170

sonsanddaughtersinternational.com
dannykittinger.com
carriekittinger.com